Inspired by Mt. Everest, th

How to Achieve Anything You Want in Life

It All Begins
With You

The Art of a Peaceful, Happy, and Healthy Life

Nem Khadge

Motivational Speaker and Certified Life Coach

How to Achieve Anything You Want in Life
It All Begins With You
The Art of a Peaceful, Happy, and Healthy Life
Nem Khadge
Motivational Speaker and Certified Life Coach

Table of Contents

The Purpose of This Book

THE PURPOSE OF this book is to enable everyone to open their inner sight using their limitless natural, inner power, in order to live better, healthier, happier, and more peaceful lives. In our daily lives, we use many conveniences such as cell phones, cars, refrigerators, etc. If we use them according to the manual, they will operate well and without problems. If we ignore the manual and use them in ways they were not intended to be used, they may not run properly. Similarly, if we do not practice activities to support our mental and physical health in our daily lives, we may not be able to develop our full potential. As a result, we may not be able to create more coherence, peace, and prosperity in our lives. This book is not just a book—it is written with a foundation of life experience. This book can serve anyone as a guide to the art of a peaceful, happy, healthy life. Reading this book will also encourage people to educate themselves about how to achieve anything they want in life.

Small actions may seem trivial to you as you go about your daily life. Understanding and practicing the knowledge and techniques I have shared in this book will make a huge difference to you, your family, the society you live in, and the whole world. We all know that action inspires us to make our lives better. My recommendation to all readers is to get inspired to make a difference in this world through your unconditional love and the action you take to serve the greater good. This book also provides a process to examine what is going on in your life right now, what your obstacles and challenges are, and what action steps you can take to help you achieve the things you've always wanted.

I would like to thank all my family members in Nepal and the US, my friends and family across the globe, all the Nepalese community from Nepal and the US, and all the IT and non-IT professionals from Nepal and the US who gave me the opportunity to learn about them and their lives, both personally and professionally. The notable lessons I have learned over twenty-five years are priceless. My real-life experiences of dealing with people with easy personalities, negative personalities, difficult personalities, and multiple personalities led me to write this book. This book will help not only to improve the reader's personal and professional development in their daily life but also to strengthen their inner power for greater coherence and work/life balance. These skills will also help to develop great relationships with anyone you come in contact with. I have seen many lives take a turn for the worse due to unpredictable and unexpected situations. This book will help you to weather life's storms.

My special thanks to my mother, Kanchhi Khadge, who showed me this beautiful planet and let me be who I always wanted to become. Special thanks to my late father, Nirmal Khadge, who encouraged me in many ways to do something for people that makes their lives easier and to consider myself a part of the world family. I am sure he is watching me now, proud that I am publishing a book to make a positive impact on others.

I would also like to extend my special thanks to my dearest wife, Nishma Khadge, who shared with me my greatest life lessons, through being my soul mate. I would not have been able to write this book without her support, love, and contribution.

Preface

I AM NOT writing this book because people know nothing about what I am going to say or because they do not understand how to manage their everyday peaceful and happy lives. I am a creative person with a sacred soul who wants to share with the world what I have learned and experienced for decades in my own personal and professional life. I am motivated by the geniuses in the world who have changed the lives of billions of people across the globe through their motivational and inspirational speeches.

"It all begins with you." This simple concept is the vital element of your daily action that will help you grow, stay healthy mentally and physically, and succeed in the rest of your life.

My writing this book is not intended as a criticism of other renowned motivational speakers and writers in the world. I don't mean to be disrespectful to what they have already proven and demonstrated. My philosophy is to help everyone to live their God-given life simply, easily, and happily with mental and physical peace. In other words, my aim is to help people live their lives with profound knowledge of the best that humans can be, because each of us has unlimited natural powers to use and apply to our daily lives. We just need to explore and work on it every single moment.

You may be wondering how I became inspired by Mt. Everest, the highest mountain in the world, to write this book. Let me explain why I am writing this book, and why this knowledge is so important to share with people all over the world.

First of all, think about the individual who determined that Mt. Everest is the highest mountain in the world. They might have had the goal of finding the world's highest mountain. When someone is inspired to see their life in a different paradigm, that person has unlimited power to achieve anything in their life. Hence, life itself encouraged someone to discover the world's highest mountain.

After Mt. Everest was declared the highest mountain in the world, many people wanted to set a world record by being the first to climb it. Many people tried, but even their formidable courage was not enough to reach the summit. Many people tried, doing their absolute best. One reason so many people failed is that when the amount of oxygen in a person's blood falls below a certain level, the heart rate soars to up to 140 beats per minute, increasing the risk of a heart attack.

Climbers have to give their bodies time to acclimate to the lung-crushing conditions in the Himalayas before attempting to summit Everest. Finally, Sir Edmund Hillary and Sherpa Tenzing Norgay were determined and continued their journey until they reached the summit. This signaled to all of humankind that there is hardly anything on earth that humans cannot do.

Sir Edmund Hillary and Tenzing Sherpa had a clear plan in place, had previous experience climbing high mountains, and had a solid entry and exit strategy in place that made them successful. Additionally, their strong motivation, willpower, and can-do attitude were the most important factors in getting them to the top of the world. As a result, these two climbers were successful because of their fearless action. They were strong mentally and physically, had a great positive attitude, a regular healthy diet, and the training needed to climb mountains. They both knew that they would surely die if they fell during their mountain-climbing expedition to the top of the world, but they took that challenge as an opportunity to set a world record. Their unstoppable imagination drove them to conquer Mt. Everest for the first time in mountain-climbing history. Their record will stand for generations to come.

In researching and analyzing many successful people around the world, all of them have one thing in common: their goals and aspirations are very precise and clear. They may change their plans, but not the destination. They do one thing at a time, with careful planning and strategy, vision, mission, and passion along with education and experience. They always keep the momentum of greatness within themselves through their actions. When they do things, they know exactly what, where, when, why, and how—and then they add willpower. They make 100% commitment and give 100% effort in the right direction at the right time. Their vision tends to emerge with consistent high self-esteem and experience. Self-esteem is one of many fundamental qualities of personal growth and achievement in life. It all begins with you.

Introduction

I'D LIKE TO tell you about the journey of my life, which inspired me to help people develop a positive attitude. It all came to me naturally, as I grew up. My late father, Nirmal Khadge (1937-2014) used to say when I was a kid, "Son, you will need to inspire others, to make a difference—but not just to make a good living. Help others as much as you can, to make this world a better place to live." My father was the kind of person who sacrificed everything for the welfare of his own family and others. One day, when he came home, I saw him get out of his car wearing only one undergarment. I asked him what had happened to his clothes. He said he gave them to poor people in a remote area who had nothing to wear. He added that he had a lot of other clothing at home that he could wear. There were many poor people in Kathmandu, Nepal in the early 1980s, within 20-30 kilometers of our suburban neighborhood. I could feel that there was more power in giving than in receiving. He used to say that giving is a process of receiving something from someone. It was a powerful statement. I didn't realize and experience that feeling until I started giving things to people when they needed something from me, in the form of financial, physical, and psychological help. I have always received more in my life than I have given to others. My attitude when giving something to someone who deserves it is that I have no expectation of being given anything in return. That frame of mind has brought me this far in life.

When I started my early childhood education, the school spelled my name "Name" by mistake. This happened because my parents used to call me "Niyem," which means "law" or "rule." People used to tease me by asking whether they would have Nem's Law. Although I was quiet by nature and didn't talk much, I used to giggle and say yes, I would have a law named after me someday. Later, when I was in elementary school, I noticed the error and had the spelling of my name corrected to "Nem," which is the correct way to write it, in the Nepalese language. In college, many of my friends were confused about my name being "Nem." After I came to the US in 1999 to get my second master's degree at Maharishi University of Management in Fairfield, Iowa, people were very curious about my name. I couldn't explain it well enough, but as I started motivating people to grow and change, personally and professionally, some people respectfully suggested that "Nem" stands for "Naturally Engaging Motivator." I liked the idea of my name standing for something more and embraced it as a full form of my name.

Let us think about life for a little bit. We all know that mankind is the pinnacle of evolution, considered to be the supreme creature in the world. Nature has given all humans what they need, but not necessarily always what they want. Humans are designed to get and become what they deserve. There are no innately good or bad people or things in the world—all value judgments are perceptions of mind, reflecting our way of thinking and perceiving things and people around us. Each of us is well aware of who we are now, and where we originated. Different people have presented various opinions and thoughts about human life. Needless to say, human mothers are the ones who give birth to all of humankind. Each mother keeps her child safely in the womb until the time arrives to come out and experience this amazing and beautiful world. We all have a history, knowing where, when, and how we were born, and how we were raised to be who we are today. But no human can directly recall the real-time experience of coming out of their mother's womb. A person can, of course, watch their own live birth video, but it is not a real memory. When we start growing through stages of age, we finally reach adulthood. We become self-reliant and learn how to survive on our own and how to make a living. That's the starting point of life. Self-reliance basically teaches us how to look to ourselves 100% of the time for all aspects of life, rather than looking to someone else for help.

Let us remember our early childhood and the important moments of the path to adulthood, to understand the what, where, when, how, and why of our life journey. There is no one, and there will never be anyone in the whole world, who knows you better than you know yourself. We have all done so many things in our lives—good or bad, right or wrong—but we did them anyway, in the past. Those days are now history, and we can't change them. Time has passed and will continue to move at its own pace into the future, without being biased toward or against anyone.

Whether child or adult, man or woman, married or un-married, educated or uneducated, rich or poor—we are each given 24 hours every day. Hence, time is very precious and unstoppable. Time is very important, because what we are today and what we will become tomorrow depend on how we use our time today. Time is a virtual essence of our lives that lets us gather information, meet people, work, and make money by using energy, and recharge through sleep and rest.

The future is uncertain and will always remain a mys-tery—it can make you feel excited or anxious. Yesterday is history that cannot be changed. Today is where we all live and do what we do. The present is the important moment to enjoy what we are given but not to waste time worrying about what we do not have. Although nature has given us everything we need, though not all we want, human life is designed to give each of us what we deserve. It is a fair, natural process for every person in the world. No one has a private sun or moon, or any other unusual natural resources. Everyone is capable of exploring and using their own hidden talents, skills, ideas, expertise, knowledge, and intelligence to make use of natural and cultivated resources to succeed in any area of life. Time is moving really fast, because we all exist on this planet as prepaid gift cards with different expiration dates. Siddhartha Gautam (the Buddha) once said, "Life is short. Time is fast. No replay. No rewind. So enjoy every moment as it comes." This is so true, and most people do not understand the value of the present moment—but if you're reading this, you've already transcended the category of "most people."

I encourage all the brilliant people of this planet who feel unimportant to identify their life purpose. It is important to clarify, envision, become passionate about, and know exactly what you want in your life. This list should be very clear and precise, so that you can identify what is most important to you without caring what other people think. Remember that others' opinions of you do not make your reality. In order to change your reality, you need to change your perspective and attitude. Factors will arise from every corner to interfere with your vision, even from your own family, but you must accept that, knowing where you want to go and what you want to become in your life. When you see that kind of vision from a positive aspect, then your family members do not want you to fail or be unsuccessful. They may express fear or doubt, but your high self-esteem, confidence, and self-reliance will see you through to achieve anything you want in your life. Along with this, you must respect your values and their importance, which will lead you to the final destination.

You must consider yourself to be a service provider in any life situation. Start with a bite-sized action toward your life passion every day. Start consistently committing to positive actions that create a peaceful, happy, and healthy life. This will help to create positive environments not only within yourself, but in your community, your society, and the whole world. Always let situations and circumstances work for you, not against you. If you're reading this and you believe you don't need these kinds of suggestions from anyone, then this isn't the book for you—but at least, try to utilize your precious time to help build a better lifestyle and healthy living habits rather than sitting in the corner complaining and being unhappy about things that cannot be changed. There are many people in the world who badly need the kind of knowledge contained in this book, which might eventually help to change someone's life. Although this book can be most beneficial to those between the ages of twenty-one and thirty-five, I hope that anyone reading it will find helpful information that will bear fruit in their lives.

Just imagine—we all have a variety of skills, knowledge, experience, and mindsets. We need to ask ourselves questions about what we could have done differently that might have created more harmony and peace, when we look back on our lives. That's the lesson we have already learned, isn't it? The past is the past and cannot be changed. There's no sense in crying over spilt milk. The past is history and tomorrow is a mystery. As I have already mentioned, that future will make you feel either excited or anxious. I have learned in life that logic might take us from Point A to Point B, or input equals output, but our imaginations and dreams, paired with real action, can take us everywhere with no limitation, no matter where we want to go and what we want to become. Without a plan, any dream will always remain a dream, unless concentrated action is put toward it. You can do anything you want or desire in your life; all you need is good initial planning, with faith, hope, and love needed to inspire you to take the right action at the right time. I often see people spending too much time on things without having a clear goal in mind. They keep complaining that they can't get where they are going, blaming situations and circumstances or other people. Some people would rather do that than take responsibility and admit to their mistakes. People want change without actually having to make any changes to themselves. As Einstein said, "Doing the same thing over and over again and expecting different results is the definition of insanity."

There have been times in our lives that, when examined, make us realize that we have done something we shouldn't have done—or conversely, that we did the right thing. My recommendation to anyone reading this book is to apply good, realistic, relevant knowledge to your daily life. We all have learned so many things through our mistakes, through many types of learning and experiences in our past lives. To err is human. We do not need to be the same people we were yesterday, if we have the guts to change our mentality and thought processes, our desires, our belief systems, and our perceptions about someone or something. We must accept things as they come, because we cannot change those things, no matter what happens in our lives. Just put a positive spin on it, let it go, and move forward with better decisions.

Because we are human, we will all make mistakes. The

important thing is to realize that making the same mistakes over and over again will not help our growth. Personal development has to be a greater priority than our current situations/problems/issues. If not, we cannot resolve those factors in our lives. We know that some people make intentional mistakes and apologize if they are caught or if the mistake is pointed out by someone else. Some even fight with others to justify their errors and say they are not mistakes. They may be right, from their perspective, but people need to look at their actions realistically and practically to measure and confirm whether they have made a genuine mistake. Sometimes people know they are doing things the wrong way but they still do those things on purpose. Those are called intentional mistakes. An unintentional mistake is something that happens due to lack of knowledge on the part of someone who is trying to accomplish or achieve something but does not do it correctly.

We all know that talk is cheap. Although it is human nature, I would not recommend or suggest that anyone recall past incidents over and over that might give you pain and sorrow or demoralize and humiliate you or push you toward destructive actions. Just develop a "can't change it" mindset. Certainly, we can recall past events, as long as we can transform such memories into positive aspects of life. It is obvious that pain is a must in our lives, to grow, progress, and learn new things. No one living on this planet is pain-free. Everyone has pain. If someone says they have no pain in life, it is a lie. Different people handle pain in different ways. However, suffering is optional. I have experienced a lot of bitter incidents in my own life, meeting and dealing with people, and sad incidents affecting other people, which I helped to resolve. At the end of the day, we cannot change anything in the past. Sometimes, people simply cannot get away from their past. I truly do have respect for that. I meet a lot of people as part of my life coach and mentorship sessions. They all have one thing in common—they say "I want peace and happiness in my life, but I am not able to concentrate." But they keep bringing all their past bitter experiences into their present life.

It's true that everyone wants happiness and peace. What many people don't seem to realize is that we cannot change the past. We just need to find the root cause of our unhappiness and work toward resolving it, on a daily basis. You need to ask yourself what makes you feel happy and peaceful. We need to make a list of everything required to create happiness and peace. Write down a step-by-step process to make things right. Once you have that list ready, start working on it in bite-sized pieces, with a clear vision every single day. For example, if you do not like the job you are doing, then find out what job you really want, and start searching for work that interests you more. At the same time, you need to prepare for your eventual job interview while searching for your new job.

We always have the choice, at any moment of our lives, to make life enjoyable, memorable, and interesting—or all miserable. We can always make our day the best it can be, or the worst—or we can just let it be a day. It really is up to us. Although it is not easy, anyone can practice making every day better, by following some simple steps. It is understandable that people find this to be difficult, and sometimes situations and circumstances are not in our favor. That is true, and yet the outcome depends on how we want to think about something and accept or reject it. I am rehashing here again that we cannot change anything from the past. It is what it is. We simply cannot change it. Also, the past cannot be changed to make a better day in the present moment. The present has its own value and momentum. No matter what we do in our lives, we must do it with grace.

In order to make a better life tomorrow, we must have a better plan today. We must start taking action with 100% commitment and effort, and move forward. We must have passion for our goals, strong willpower, and a clear vision of what, where, when, how, and why to do certain things in our lives that will eventually lead us to a fulfilling, successful future.

People have different perspectives about striving for a satisfying life vs. a successful life. Some say a successful life is better, because success is quantifiable and measured by others. For myself, I prefer a satisfying life, because it is measured by my own soul, mind, and heart that create emotions to nurture my peace. What we see and how we feel about ourselves and others comes from our perceptions and thought processes. You don't have to agree with me on this, if you prefer a successful life rather than a satisfied life. It's an individual preference.

Einstein once said that nothing can travel faster than the speed of light. But things have changed in the 21st century. When my son Niral was in the seventh grade, he said, "Dad, the speed of human thought is faster than anything in the world today." However, there is a lot of scientific research on this topic. In support of this point, I'd like to quote from the October 2011 issue of *Popular Science* magazine:

"Yes, the universe itself will eventually outpace the speed of light. Just how this will happen is a bit complicated, so let's begin at the very beginning: the big bang. Around 14 billion years ago, all matter in the universe was thrown in every direction. That first explosion is still pushing galaxies outward. Scientists know this because of the Doppler effect, among other reasons. The wavelengths of light from other galaxies shift as they move away from us, just as the pitch of an ambulance siren changes as it moves past.

Take Hydra, a cluster of galaxies about three billion light years away. Astronomers have measured the distance from the Earth to Hydra by looking at the light coming from the cluster. Through a prism, Hydra's hydrogen looks like four strips of red, blue-green, blue-violet and violet. But during the time it takes Hydra's light to reach us, the bands of color have shifted down toward the red end—the low-energy end—of the spectrum. On their journey across the universe, the wavelengths of light have stretched. The farther the light travels, the more stretched it gets. The farther the bands shift toward the red end, the farther the light has traveled. The size of the shift is called the redshift, and it helps scientists figure out the movement of stars in space. Hydra isn't the only distant cluster of galaxies that displays a redshift, though. Everything is shifting, because the universe is expanding. It's just easier to see Hydra's redshift because the farther a galaxy is from our own, the faster it is moving away.

There is no limit to how fast the universe can expand, says physicist Charles Bennett of Johns Hopkins University. Einstein's theory that nothing can travel faster than the speed of light in a vacuum still holds true, because space itself is stretching, and space is nothing. Galaxies aren't moving through space and away from each other but with space—like raisins in a rising loaf of bread. Some galaxies are already so far away from us, and moving away so quickly, that their light will never reach Earth. 'It's like running a 5K race, but the track expands while you're running,' Bennett says. 'If it expands faster than you can run, you'll never get where you're going.'"

Let's talk about what makes people embrace change in their lives. Does it require courage, talent, wealth, or emotion to make people open to change? There may be thousands of answers to this question. However, I feel it is important for everyone to understand the basic traditional senses of the human body: Sight, Hearing, Smell, Taste, and Touch—we usually refer to these five, even though people really have seven including Vestibular and Proprioception. Needless to say, each sensory organ associated with each sense sends information to the brain, to help people understand and perceive the world around them.

It all begins with you, as you were born an ordinary person on this planet. We each have 24 hours a day, no matter what, where, when, how, and why we do things. Certainly, we can make more money with hard work and dedication, but there is no way for us to make more time, no matter what we want to do in our lives. Time is the most unstoppable, most precious gift ever given to us by nature. It is our choice whether to make good use of it or just let it pass by. It does not require anyone's permission to keep it rolling, and no one can stop it, either. It is our choice whether to utilize or waste 86,400 seconds, every day. It is like currency—once you spend it, it's gone forever.

I have divided *It All Begins With You* into multiple categories of daily activity that will help anyone to understand how they can live the life they want. I am sure that we all want to be more energetic, healthy, happy, fulfilled, and peaceful in our lives. The biggest question is how we can make this happen. The first step is to be able to manage and control our daily activities of mental and physical health in the most effective and efficient ways. Without self-discipline, this goal cannot be achieved. People have a tendency to do the same thing over and over, expecting a different result. But you will never have a different result until and unless you take different action. The short answer is that your life is all about you—your feelings, your emotions, your consciousness, your actions, and the results of each action you have taken. Here are some secrets you might want to take into consideration as you read through this book.

Understanding Human Needs

SINCE WE EVOLVE as humans after we are born, our needs are different, depending on our priorities and focus during each phase and in each area of life. Eventually, we must serve and fulfill our lives as a whole.

We cannot deny that we can't survive without food, water, shelter, and sleep. Someone might say, "What about oxygen and the sun?" That's a fair point, but those things exist naturally, without anyone having to find them. I am talking about resources we have to create or be given. As we become adults, sex can be added to the list of human needs.

Human life is fueled by needs and runs by itself, regardless of how long we live or how we live our lives. It is important how we focus on living the life gifted to us by Nature. I often tell people that there is no guarantee of anything in life, regardless of whether we live for the next 60 seconds or the next 60 years. It's beyond our control. Let us briefly talk here about some human needs.

Safety and Security: When we are born, we seek safety and security from our mothers. We cry until our mothers hold us. That makes us feel comfortable, safe, and secure. We absolutely do what is needed to help life run smoothly, happily, and peacefully on a day-to-day basis.

Variety: As humans, we want to do something different from what we have been doing for years. For example, if we spend all day every day at work, it is good to take a little time, go to a park, and feel and experience natural beauty.

You can spend time with family, exploring different activities. Meet people in your community with different cultural backgrounds, race, or nationality and learn something from them. Look for adventure and get a whole new level of life experience. Your choices will be determined by what makes you and your companions feel good. Some people like hiking, some like travel—others like climbing mountains, writing, dancing, etc. All it takes to have an adventure is the three I's: Interest, Initiation, and Implementation. This is something I learned from my eldest brother, Nir R Khadge, twenty-five years ago.

Significance: We are all special on this planet. When you do something, do it with your heart and soul, and give valuable service to others. This is how you add significance to your life, and how you make others feel that you are valuable to them. If you want to be seen as "great," then you must perform great actions. Many people never want to go above and beyond—that is why they live in mediocrity. In my experience, actions speak louder than words, in any situation. We are talking here about how important we are to someone, or vice versa. Appreciation and recognition are gained as your significance, in acknowledgment of your great contribution and support to someone or something, which made a difference.

Love, Affection, and Human Connection: Love, affection, and human connection are the other major needs of human beings. We see a lot of human connection these days through social media such as Facebook, Twitter, Instagram, YouTube, and other networking platforms. However, we are missing love and affection. We have all learned arithmetic at school. We know that when you have something and you give it to someone, then it's gone. Love and affection, though, multiply when you give them away, and they continue to grow from there. Love and affection can melt the heart even of selfish and cruel individuals, but it takes many years of practice to understand and realize what unconditional love really is. Once you understand it, you will be able to accept and give unconditional love and affection.

When you teach yourself how to love and take care of yourself first, then you will know how to love others and take care of their needs. Love is a natural, emotional, unconditional silent language that only your heart can hear, speak, and explain and only your soul can understand, feel, and realize. Love and affection are powerful when we give them to someone, with respect and kindness.

I see many people who do not care for themselves, but they do take care of others just to let their community and the world know about it. The good works they do are not something they want to do in their heart and soul—they just want to do it and get it over with. I see a lack of love and affection in their actions. Many times, I see that they are just hungry to show off their unsolicited contribution to family, friends, and society without taking care of their own health. By the same token, some family members do not take care of themselves. They do not maintain their health with good diet and exercise, and they don't even take their prescribed medicines correctly. They stay busy working, every single day. They even keep track of the time they spend at work and talk about it, so they can prove to people how hard they are working to make a good living for their family. But what's the point of working so hard that you can't take care of your own well-being? Those people don't want to be around others; they prefer to stay alone and be self-centered. Yes, we all need to work to make a living. That does not mean we should ignore our health or take time away from family—or not spend time with them even when we can, especially with our partner and children.

Growth: In order to experience this world as a better place to live, we must grow through our experience, knowledge, love, affection, and human connection with others. The nature of life is to grow, no matter how we live our lives. When we do good things every day, we strengthen our life, and that goodness becomes our habit. Similarly, if we do bad things every day, we strengthen evil, and that becomes a habit, too. When we practice something, it grows, and growth does not distinguish between good and bad. I would strongly recommend to anyone who wants to experience better mental and physical health that you should seek progress in your emotional, intellectual, and spiritual life. Your progress reflects where you spend most of your time.

Family/Social Contribution: This is the most important part of life. When we know how to support ourselves economically, financially, socially, and spiritually, then we must learn to contribute something to others, to make a difference. It begins with us first, and then moves on to our family. Contributing to family means helping yourself and your immediate family members. Then, you can move on and support other family members as much as you can. For example, your grandfather may need money for medical treatment that he cannot afford. If you are in a position to help him, you should. But to do that, you must be financially stable. Then you can contribute to society by setting up a charity that can help change someone's life. For example, the Khadge family has set up a school charity fund in Nepal, where the poorest student in each grade receives a scholarship every year.

Even if you don't have the physical or financial resources to provide significant help, you can always brighten someone's day with a kind word or a smile, or spend ten minutes to help someone with a task that will make a difference to their lives. That is what I call a life worth living.

Identify Yourself

WHEN I SAY "identify yourself," what I mean is that you should understand who you really are; what your life purpose is; what makes you feel great, inspired, extraordinary, and valued; what you are very good at doing, naturally and spontaneously; and what passion you have for doing things that make you feel happy and fulfilled. I believe that there is a lot more to life than we usually see. The majority of people are inspired only by the opportunity to make more money.

You may experience this in a different paradigm if there are more reasons to live differently than you are currently living—and there are many reasons. Anyone can become a better version of themselves, because they can achieve more than they already have. This kind of attitude will shift your life to the next level if you start working on it without further delay. It takes time to feel, experiment, and realize in any area of life. The question you must ask yourself is where and how your time is being spent. I can tell you from my experience that at least half of your free time is used for entertainment. I am not saying we do not need entertainment, but we need to observe reasonable limits. It is prudent to understand the value of time. If you really want to become who you have dreamed of becoming, I recommend using your time wisely.

What I can tell you is that your life is your dream. You are the director of your own life. As you grow, you will start writing your own scripts for your life. Those scripts get added into your personal profile, every day. If you keep adding scripts, it will eventually become a movie of your life, which can be a symbol of success. The question to ask yourself is whether you want to make a movie of miscellaneous scenes, or a movie with a specific theme that inspires others. We all have experienced in our lives situations in which someone told us what to do, where to do it, when, how, and why. If we keep doing what others have suggested, then we become what they want us to become. Is that really what you want? We become what we practice most. So, just be specific about what you ultimately want to become in your life. You must demand it. Being a unique personality in the world, you must identify yourself and believe in yourself. When you believe in yourself, those around you will start believing in you, too. If you need anything in your life and you do not believe in yourself, then you are unlikely to succeed. There is nothing more important in this world than discovering and expressing your identity.

Regardless of our belief system and background, each of us has only one life with one mind, one heart, and one soul. We learn what, where, when, how, and why to do things, but we must also develop our willpower and cultivate "want to do" and "can do" attitudes. You want to be able to look at yourself in the mirror every single morning and feel proud of yourself because what you see was, ultimately, made by you. If you have a stain on your face and you do not see it, cleaning the mirror won't make it go away. We know that what you look like is important to some, but the ultimate importance is how you appear to yourself inside, from your heart and soul.

Whether you have been stuck or made progress in your life, you have answers to all of those questions when you start interacting with your inner life. It also helps with self-study and self-development. Knowing who you are in your life is the foremost important value of your unique humanity in this world. Even though people say we are born geniuses, the beginning of life is the same for everyone. It's not until later that life starts to evolve, influenced by life stage and environment. Eventually, each person becomes ordinary or exceptional, based on the environment and situations they grow up with. It does not matter who you were or who you are today—what really matters is who you can be. It is always possible for you to be the best version of yourself, if you are committed to it.

Who you are today will impact your surroundings, and it all begins with you. In my experience, if we live with or spend time around negative and cynical people, we will be affected. It is important to remember that our thoughts are like seeds, and our mind is fertile ground. The mind does not care what we plant in it in the form of a thought—it will always yield results. Since we can plant either happiness or misery into our minds, it is up to us to plant what we really want to grow.

First things first: energy flows toward and grows whatever we put our attention on. As soon as you open your eyes in the morning, create the good intention of getting excited about your day and getting excited about your life. Express your gratitude to nature, and compliment yourself, saying that it's another great day to be alive on this planet. What I mean here is that you must learn an attitude of gratitude. This means that we should be grateful for all the blessings we have in our lives. The equation of blessings is home plus family and love. Be grateful for the place where you dwell. Be grateful for everything and everyone surrounding you. It could be just you along with your partner, spouse, kids, and family members—or it could be anyone from your community and society.

One way to express your gratitude to others is to show respect to and honor those who have helped you in many ways to grow and develop in your life. You can express that gratitude in many ways, such as by talking on the phone, texting, emailing, or even writing a traditional letter or returning a personal favor. Just ensure that you have great respect for all of them, as well as for what you have been given in your valuable day-to-day life. Realize that things could be worse. Feel in yourself that nature is creating great moments to deal with for the rest of the day, as your day has just begun.

Before your day starts, you can make a list of three to five of the most important things that are must-do action items before heading out to work. Get your schedule organized for the day—that will make you feel like the rest of your day is a great journey. Keep in mind that things already planned may not go exactly as you envision them. People whom you believe to be good may not always live up to your expectations. Just be prepared to be patient, flexible, and easy to work with, no matter who you are dealing with.

People sometimes like to gossip and talk about others. It is normal to have positive and negative thoughts about people—we just need to learn how to handle those thoughts. It's human nature to talk about both the positive and negative aspects of others. I know sometimes it can cause hurt feelings when a lot of negative things are said about you or someone else. The question should really be asked whether that conversation can be changed after it has already ended. The answer is no. It's human nature to find it difficult to get away from negative thoughts. One thing I've learned in life is to let go of things I can't change. In my late teens, I started having trouble handling those kinds of situations. I taught myself that I could not change the past, and I couldn't change what other people thought or said about me, and vice versa. I applied those experiences to my life and embraced the concept of letting bygones be bygones. When I started doing this, I really questioned myself. It wasn't easy. Initially, it was not fun to question myself all the time. Later, I embraced it as a regular habit when I felt frustrated and low. I used to wake up early in the morning and start asking myself "why" questions. Eventually, after many years of practice, I found the answers to all of those questions.

When anything happens in life, it's always 50/50 involvement, meaning that 50% of issues or concerns come from you, and the other 50% come from someone or somewhere else. Let me give you an example. Let us say someone came to you and started arguing about the quality of a task you just performed. In this scenario, if you hadn't performed that task, there wouldn't be an issue. Another example is someone saying something about you, and wanting to argue with you on that topic. You might say that you didn't do anything. To illustrate this scenario—it takes an average of 8 minutes 20 seconds for light to travel from the sun to the earth. The sun has already risen, but its light won't appear on earth until later. In this scenario, you might have said something to someone without the intention of conveying that message to others in a way that caused your name to be involved. Now, someone is making up a story about your saying something to someone, and the issue came with your involvement. There must be a cause, to see the effect. This is related to the philosophy of action and reaction. Remember that you cannot change anyone on this planet, but you can change yourself. When you do so, that will influence other people to change. There are some people who do not want to change, and you need to just let them be on their own. All I know from my experience is that life is full of surprises, pain, and blessings. Things always change. People change, on both practical and impractical levels. But you can always stay yourself, if you want. You have the choice to stay true to yourself, being kind and helpful. Also, you have other choices, whether you do or do not want to sacrifice who you are for anyone who really needs your love, compassion, cooperation, and support in their lives.

Sometimes, you are confronted by difficult circumstances despite not having done anything to anyone. The problem is that when you are connected with many people as part of your community, society, or network, it's not always easy to stay in touch with everyone whom you have known for many years. On the other hand, people do not realize that everyone has their own lives to take care of, and their daily needs. There is no lack of people who are just envious and unhappy no matter what you do or how you do it. How someone is treated by people other than you is beyond your control. We know that we are often treated the same way that we treat others, but if you are treated badly, you do not need to do unto others what has been done unto you. If you retaliate, there is no difference between you and the person who wronged you. For that reason, there are situations where you should not treat others as you have been treated. From your end, you can control yourself, if you try. You cannot shut off people who say things about you—whether good or bad. We all like to have only good things said about us. But what you can do is control yourself, and stay quiet if you hear something bad being said about you. Don't spend energy on defending yourself—that energy can be spent in so many other creative ways. Certainly, there are times when you may need to take immediate action to prevent such an incident from happening again, but you need to learn how to handle such things in a positive way, without creating more issues.

Be aware that some people enjoy interfering with others' lives, whether intentionally or unintentionally. The most important thing for anyone to learn is how to communicate with others without interrupting what they are doing at that point in time. For example, a wife and husband are talking about a serious matter and an adult family member interrupts and starts talking about something else without asking whether this is a good time. There is always a way to communicate without being disruptive. It's important that we give people privacy and space to spend time on their own.

As part of my work as a couples counselor, I met Raghu and Radha, who had a normal life. They gave permission for me to discuss their story in this book, to help other people learn from their example. One day, Radha's mother decided to visit. They welcomed her, and everything was fine for the first few weeks. But one day, Raghu realized that his time with his wife and children had been reduced due to his mother-in-law, although he was a caring individual who loved his family. But Radha and her mother would talk until midnight almost every day. When Raghu returned from work, they would serve him dinner, but the husband and wife had almost no private time together. By the time Radha came to bed, Raghu would already be asleep. Typically, after Raghu came home from work, he would help with the kids' schoolwork and other activities. Previously, his wife would keep him company and be engaged with the kids as well.

Finally, Raghu asked his wife to cut back on the time she spent talking to her mother and suggested she spend more time with him and the kids. She took this the wrong way, got angry, and said she would not do it. Raghu let it go. On another occasion, Raghu got home from the office and saw his wife and mother-in-law talking. They didn't pay any attention to him when he came home. Raghu called his wife into another room and they had a little argument, because his wife had not spent time with him ever since her mother came to stay. His wife told him not to be jealous of the time she spent with her mother. Raghu reminded her that she had an obligation to care for her husband and kids as well as talking to her mother all day long, which was ruining the family's life. She said she enjoyed spending time with her mother, and that he should not be jealous.

One day, Raghu was working from home. His wife was taking a shower, and while she was out of earshot, he spoke to his mother-in-law and asked her to spare Radha some time during the day rather than talking to her all day long. She told Radha that Raghu didn't like them talking. Radha got really upset and angry with her husband. Raghu knew she was upset and asked if she was okay. She started to cry and said he could have told her directly to stop spending so much time with her mother. She blamed him for upsetting her mother. The issue was that Raghu had only the best intentions when he communicated with his mother-in-law, and he didn't know that she would take the message back to Radha with bad intent. Raghu learned that he couldn't trust his mother-in-law.

Later, Raghu's mother-in-law came to tell him bad things about Radha, while Radha was dropping her daughter at school. Raghu didn't want to tell Radha what had happened, as he knew it would negatively affect Radha's relationship with her mother. Raghu didn't want to cause that kind of problem with his wife, after they had been married for more than eighteen years. After a few days, Raghu overheard his mother-in-law complaining about him to Radha. She did not realize that her own son was not contributing to her support, whereas Raghu was tirelessly taking care of many personal

and health needs for her and her family. He always appreciated the household work she did to help Radha, but he didn't
appreciate her behavior, which could lead to breaking up
her daughter's own family. One day, Raghu and Radha had
a small argument. Radha's mother jumped in to say Radha
should pack her bags and come with her mother to India.
Raghu was very surprised by this cruel language and unexpected behavior.

A few months later, when he was worn out from dealing
with Radha and her mother, a friend recommended that he
talk to me. Raghu explained to me that there was no longer
any privacy between him and Radha because his wife would
share all private conversations with her mother, and he needed some advice from me about what to do in order to keep his
family life healthy. It was sad to hear all his stories, but things
couldn't be changed. He didn't want to damage his relationship with Radha, due to a promise he had made to his father-
in-law. One day, I invited Raghu into my office. I gave him
some specific instructions about what, where, when, how, and
why to take action to fix the broken relationship with Radha
and his mother-in-law. I asked Raghu if he could bring Radha
to my office on a weekly basis. He agreed, and I met with
them once a week to assess their progress. They both made a
commitment and strictly followed my recommendations.

After a few weeks of hard work and dedication, they
made great progress and started leading a normal life again.
They were able to fix their broken relationship. They learned
valuable lessons from their own experience. They both realized and worked to correct their weaknesses and flaws. They
started sharing information with each other every day and
never allowed a third person to come between them. Radha
learned a lesson about not sharing private things with her

mother or with anyone else. Raghu learned so many things about his mother-in-law—not even his wife knew her better. Radha started a new career in IT and kept herself busy. They were back to a happy journey, leading a normal life with their three beautiful kids.

In order to avoid future fights with his daughter and son-in-law, Radha's father made a phone call to Radha's mother from India, and reminded her that she should not interfere in their daughter's life. After a few days, Radha's father urgently asked his wife to return to India for good, and she flew home. Radha's father had a small business, and her mother started helping him. Radha's mother rarely calls her these days, because she feels guilty about trying to ruin her daughter's happy life. The moral is that anyone can certainly visit family, but they must respect the privacy and rights of other people. It takes years of work to fix broken relationships.

As part of my mentorship to others, I meet with a lot of couples having issues in their married lives. I find one of the reasons is that people do not communicate well and try to hide things from each other. Besides, some people are very self-centered and prefer to focus on their individual needs as a priority in every aspect of life, but they don't really care deeply about their own spouse or children. They live together as husband and wife just to fit in with society. What they do not understand is that society won't help them to stay healthy and happy in their lives. They need to work with one another to fix their problems, but often, they choose instead to complain to a third party about their family life. If that third party is a counselor, motivator, or mentor (like me), then they will get good, constructive advice to fix the issues and prevent the relationship from getting worse. Complaining and saying bad things about your spouse to someone outside your relationship isn't the way to keep your relationship healthy. I have seen dozens of marriages end in divorce due to these kinds of situations. From my life coaching experience, I would recommend that people seek professional help immediately, if there are ongoing issues with family life. Do not wait too long, hoping that somehow your issues will resolve by themselves—they won't.

Here is an interesting story someone told me in the past, as part of my mentorship. The people in the story have authorized me to write about their experience. A woman, Jill, thought it was the right thing to do to take care of her sister, Jessica, who needed support mentally, physically, and financially. She had been making progress for the past few years; she had a job and was living with another family member, Kim, in a different city.

The problem with Jessica was that she could not deal with her family. She used to recall past incidents and blame her family for anything that went wrong in her life. One day, Jill got a call from Kim, asking her to take care of Jessica for a while. Jill agreed and brought Jessica to live with her. Jill's husband, Joe, didn't want that, because his parents were already living with them. However, Joe's parents were compassionate and encouraged Joe to support his sister-in-law. As time went by, Joe's parents and Jessica built a great relationship. She was improving in many ways, as Jill was there to help her whenever she needed support.

Joe's parents planned to move to Arizona during the winter. So they did. After they left, Jessica was on her own a lot of the time. She would read books and watch motivational videos. She started lending Jill a hand with housekeeping. When Joe and Jill went to work, she would prepare lunch and dinner for the family, including the three kids. Jessica was busy all day long in the kitchen, in the house, and taking care of her niece and nephews.

Joe was a very negative-minded individual. He would not listen to others. He had some attitude and ego problems. He had problems with his coworkers and could not get along with them. In addition to that, he wasn't very involved with his family. Jill, on the other hand, was well educated and socially respected. She would help anyone as much as possible without getting herself in trouble. When Jill would make practical suggestions to Joe, he would get mad at her. Joe liked things to be a specific way. The reason Jill wanted Jessica to live with her was that Jessica had not cared well for herself in the past. She had ruined her life with drugs, for many years. One day, one of Jessica's sisters, Kim, was informed that Jessica needed some family support. Kim decided to bring Jessica into her house to take care of her. Kim found Jessica a job, where she was doing well. It took a long time for Jessica to adjust to Kim's family. Kim decided to send her to Jill's, hoping that Jessica would listen to Jill—and she did.

One day, Jill told Joe that she would like to help Jessica find her own place in the same city where Joe and Jill lived. Joe immediately rejected the idea and said he couldn't support her for the rest of his life. He said he was married to Jill, not to her sister. Joe didn't realize that Jill had been taking care of Joe's parents physically and supporting the rest of the family for several years, rather than taking care of her own parents. It was unpleasant for Jill to confront Joe about Jessica. Since Jill was a laid-back person, she just let it go. Joe told Jill that if Jessica wanted to be around them, then Jill would end up running to help her anytime Jessica had a problem. He finally said that he would give money to support Jessica if she moved somewhere else, but that he would not keep her in the same city, at any cost. If Jill made the decision to keep Jessica in the same city, he would leave the house and family. Jill was in a trap, torn between whether to save her own family life with the kids or let go of Jessica, who was in need of her support. Joe's idea was to make Jessica independent, which was a great idea, but he didn't realize that in order for her to succeed, she needed to stay close by. Jill was hoping that if Jessica stayed in the same city, she would be able to find a supportive partner and launch a real life, because she had come a long way and done a lot of work on herself.

Jessica started working at a grocery store as a cashier, while living with Jill and her family. One day, she started dating Jack, a nice man who was introduced to her by a longtime mutual friend. They got to know each other through FaceTime and video chat. Jack fell in love with her. After a two-month affair, they got married. Now, they live in the same city where Jill and her family live. Part of my mentorship of Jill was resolving her damaging relationship with Joe, due to Jessica's coming into their lives. I met with each of them separately, and they were very cooperative about providing all the information to fix their issues. They are doing very well. Joe learned a lot of lessons after attending six mentorship classes with me. Jill and Joe have a better relationship than they had before. Joe has been a decent man who now understands a lot about his life purpose as a human being. He now runs to help anyone he can, when help is needed. He shares his stories with others, to encourage them to live better lives every day.

To sum up, you cannot simply ignore family members who need your love and support in order to progress and change. The person who needs help could be someone from your side of the family or your spouse's family. Keeping your loved ones too far away will make it harder to help them when they need you. Helping someone to progress and be independent is the opportunity of a lifetime. Even a moment's smile can change someone's whole day. Realize that if your spouse takes care of a lot of things for your parents and the rest of the family, then it also becomes your responsibility to take care of their needs. Love and physical support can't be traded for money. There is no guarantee that people will remain strong physically and mentally, lifelong. It is more important how we live our lives, vs. how long we live. Changes in our lives are natural, but the improvements and progress we make are what we need to focus and work on every single day. It is a way of raising the bar on your standard way of doing things. In my own words: *Success is the accumulation of every little thing you put into action every single day in order to accomplish something, with the payoff in the future.* Be aware of where you spend most of your time every day. That will determine who you become.

Another thing to learn in life is that even those who are close to you may want some space to be on their own. We expect people to give of themselves endlessly, without realizing what they might need. We just let them handle things on their own unless we need to get involved with what they are doing. In these situations, communication is key and plays a role of partnership to keep both parties on the same page. There are many incidents that could be easily solved if people had open communication rather than simply assuming that they know what others think. Sometimes, what we see as clear or good doesn't appear that way to others. It depends on how the other person sees and feels it. One thing to keep in mind is that there will never be a shortage of negative people around us. They can be anywhere. Don't get me wrong here—I am just being realistic, based on my own experience.

People are not born positive-minded or negative-minded. These attitudes evolve due to environment, professional and social networks, and circles of positive and negative people around them. Sometimes, people are affected by a positive or negative group bias. If someone is surrounded by many people with a positive attitude, that will affect people around them as well. My best suggestion is to stay away from people who tend to talk a lot about negativity and who demonstrate a negative attitude. The best approach is to minimize the time you spend with those who have a pessimistic attitude. You might want to spend more than 66% of your social time (defined as the amount of time you allocate in a week to social interaction) with someone at or above your level of positivity.

Staying around negative people will hinder your personal growth. You can definitely become a strongly negative person. We have many ways to get in touch with people regarding their relationship to us. We can create a different category for them to determine how they fit into our network of connection—we can choose to spend a minute, an hour, a day, a week, a month, a year . . . or just once in a while . . . with them. The most important thing is to create a positive family environment in your home first, and it all begins with you. Believe it or not, we are the problem—and we are the solution, too. Sometimes, you cannot change anything; circumstances may be out of your control. Change becomes the responsibility of each family member. When someone takes full responsibility for their life, that demonstrates maturity. One family member cannot change the mentality of the whole family. Shared responsibility is needed to create a good, healthy family atmosphere.

I have seen many people who simply love to interfere in others' personal and professional lives without their permission. People tend to cross boundaries in their good relationships—personal, professional, family, social, etc. Eventually, they end up damaging their good relationships. It takes years to rebuild a broken relationship, but it can be ruined in a matter of minutes. If you really want your relationships to be long-lasting, you do not want to hang back and criticize. You need to be active and consistent in your good behavior, with respect and a positive attitude. In order to win someone's trust, they expect certain things from your communication, and you must know when and how to convey your message. It is also important that you do not forget to appreciate what they have to say.

Sometimes, people think a broken relationship cannot be repaired, because that's how they feel about someone saying bad things about them. In order to handle those situations in life, people can take simple precautions, such as staying away from those who have time to talk negatively about others. Their everyday task becomes just talking about others, back-biting, etc. It is important that you keep yourself busy so that people don't get a chance to bother you by talking about something you don't want to hear about. You just need to spend more time on your passion. For example, if you love music, study and practice music. If you are a teacher, study and practice your teaching skills. If you like being an actor, study and spend more time acting, or do whatever makes you feel fulfilled and happy in your life. These kinds of habits not only make you feel good about yourself being busy; they also give you peace of mind, because you are able to do something you choose, and you don't have to listen to anything that you don't need to know about.

I understand there are cases where people simply will not stop gossiping. I call it a kind of mental disease, when people do not understand why someone may not have time to listen to their unnecessary chatter. They simply think it will heal their emotions, if they express their thoughts and experiences to someone else. Yes, sometimes it might help to heal a bad experience, if thoughts are shared. At this point, my experience is that people who are willing to share their thoughts must recognize someone who is more willing to listen. That person can be you. You are a better judge of knowing whom to listen to and in what capacity, and how to deal with such people. Your one mistake, telling someone else's story, can change their whole life.

If you need counseling, it is always advisable to find a counselor or confidant with a positive attitude or positive vibe who really knows what to share and what not to share with any third party after listening to your story. Sometimes people speak well of others, and sometimes they do not. It's none of your business, unless it has a direct connection to who you are and what you do with it after listening to it. People are different in this world. After someone says something, then others start creating a lot of thoughts about them. In my opinion, it is just a waste of time and energy.

This reminds me of something I learned from the Greek philosopher, Socrates, when I was a kid. A man rushed to Socrates and wanted to tell him something. Socrates smiled and said he would listen if the man could answer "Yes" to three simple questions. The first question was: "Is what you are going to tell me all truthful?" The man replied that he was not sure. The second question was: "Do you know whether the person involved was doing a good thing in the scenario you want to describe?" The man didn't know. The third question was: "Do I have anything to do with it, or will it be of any use to me to know this information?" The answer was no. Then Socrates walked away, saying, "The thing you were going to tell me could not be confirmed as truth. You could not confirm whether the action you would describe was performed for a good reason. Also, the message you were going to convey has no relevance to me." In reality, people tell you so many things. It is not important to listen to all of them, unless there is a reason for you to listen.

Our thoughts come either from some source of information or past experience, or some sort of belief system. It is natural to demonstrate thoughts in creating perception, assumption, showing attitudes, performing actions, demonstrating habits, showing personality, and enacting destiny. No matter who comes to communicate with us on any matter, if we must listen to them, there are three ways to handle any kind of conversation: 1) Reflect the same energy back, whether you are insulted or appreciated; 2) Absorb the energy/pain and do not say or do anything with it or feel appreciated in praising; 3) Transform the energy, have a big smile on your face, and say nothing. You can certainly wish a blessing on the person if you want to. I would recommend #3, because you cannot change anything that has already happened, and you can't take back words that have already been spoken. That blessing you gave to someone else will eventually come back to you. Blessings will not flow by themselves until we bless someone. It's the law of sowing and reaping. As you sow, so shall you reap. The seeds of an apple tree grow only apple trees, not orange trees.

Teaching yourself to be a great human, to be unstoppable and expand your mental and physical health, takes years of practice. Now, you have an opportunity. You may meet many different kinds of people in your life. You deal with people who have negative attitudes, short tempers, who are jealous, arrogant, compassionate, loving, caring, difficult to work with, kind, selfish, cruel—even those with multiple personalities. In order to deal with those people, you need to develop a fearless courage. Always be receptive and accept what they say and how they treat you, because you cannot change them. Do some study and research around these kinds of good or bad people, and learn their true character. This kind of due diligence will help you to understand new people with similar character traits, in a short period of time. In this way, you can avoid people whose unpleasant personalities you have already learned about. I can tell you from experience that when we do not respect others—their thoughts, skills, and talents— then we are not respected for our talents, either. You will be treated in the same way that you treat others. Exceptions are always out there, but we do not have control over them. I would simply pray for them to become decent people.

I have often found with some people that their words do not translate into their actions. They say many good things at social gatherings, seminars, conferences, or in big meetings, but in reality, only a few people keep their word and demonstrate that their words translate into actions. Don't get me wrong—there may be some tendency to make things happen, but that's not the case all the time. Sometimes, they intentionally care less about others' needs, feelings, and situations and they try to pull away from fulfilling their commitments and responsibilities. Along with that, they do not value others' expertise, time, and effort. For example, sometimes people require you to drive an hour to a business or personal meeting, and then they do not show up despite your having made a commitment. In reality, the person who was waiting for the meeting could have been told that the other person couldn't make it, but that person didn't take the time to be considerate.

Of course, an emergency is an exception, and everyone understands that. The person who never showed up could call after a few days to apologize, but he does not. Sometimes, people do not even bother admitting their mistakes. They don't care about valuing others' time and their commitments. Those kinds of people do not want to change, and no one can change them.

In my lifetime, I have had the opportunity to meet and work with the best of the best people, and those who have the potential to be the best people in the world. What I have learned from them is that there are three levels of people: high level, medium level, and low level.

High-level people learn from the mistakes made by others and try not to make those same mistakes in their lives. They are very rare. People from the medium level are those who make mistakes in their lives and do not repeat the same mistakes again. Most of us fall into this level. People at a low level are those who don't care about personal growth and progress. They do not want to change anything in their lives. They want to be the same person all the time—mentally, physically, socially, financially, and spiritually. They do not want to change.

We will meet both successful and unsuccessful people in our lives. It does not matter who they are—we need to learn from both positive and negative people. Positive people will teach us what to do and negative people will teach us what not to do, in order to succeed. A wise person always observes carefully, without missing anything that is going on around him, and he/she learns from there. You just need to keep your eye on the person who saw things, in order to make things happen. Paying attention to their idea can help you change your life in no time. Practice helps people advance their skills to the next level. We are all given 24 hours in a day. One fundamental aspect of managing your time is to understand that $8 + 8 + 8 = 24$. We all have 24 hours in a day. Although it is not easy to apply, you may be able to manage at least two hours of personal time every day for yourself. For example: 8-10 hours of work, 7-8 hours of sleep, 2-4 hours for family or personal time. It is up to every individual to make this happen. If you keep practicing every single day, trying to manage your time wisely, then it will likely become habitual. You just need to believe in yourself. When you believe in yourself, everyone else in the world will believe in you, too.

In order to grow, you must be passionate about your goals. Your passion will guide you toward areas of improvement. For that, you must put together a game plan in writing, and operate from there. You may need to refine your game plan if there are major changes. You must direct massive effort in the right direction. The timeline is essential, as well, meaning that time will help you to gather information and meet individuals who can help you with advice, money, and energy to make things happen. For example, water cannot fill a bucket with a hole in the bottom. We need to be aware of the process of action taken while we are trying to achieve our goals.

Always learn something new about someone or something. This will help you to expand to the next level of knowledge. It's not like the olden days, when we had to rely on radio, local newspapers, or talking to someone in person. These days, you can learn a lot of educational information through the internet, YouTube, television, etc. You can learn literally anything you want to know about, via the technology available in the modern world.

As part of your personal or professional development, I would strongly recommend that you read the many well-respected books that help you to grow mentally, physically, socially, financially, and spiritually. When you focus on a thought, the thought creates a chemical in the body. The chemical can be positive or negative. Happiness and sadness result from the chemicals that you create in your body. In one research study, a rattlesnake was used as an execution method for criminals on death row. One day, the criminal was blindfolded. He had been told he would be bitten by a rattlesnake, but instead, the executioners poked two pins into his feet. The criminal thought he had been bitten, and the fear-based chemicals produced by his body mimicked the snake's venom, causing his death. The way we feel about things in our life creates the matching chemicals in the body. Researchers have found that the human body produces at least sixty different chemicals.

Even if you are very busy, I highly recommend that you read at least one good book per month. If possible, read before going to bed. The ideal choice would be a book relevant to your passions and interests, which motivates you to do what you love most in your life.

Set Your Goals

TO ACHIEVE ANYTHING in life, we must set goals. The goals must be in writing and must be reviewed on a daily or weekly basis in order to be specific enough to hit your targeted milestone. Having goals and achieving them will greatly influence our self-esteem, which impacts others around us. When we start believing in ourselves and demonstrating that through our actions, everyone else in the world will believe in us as well. Goals can be set up in two ways: long-term and short-term.

Long-term goals are aspirations for the five, ten, twenty, or even thirty years from now. It takes about five years, or ten thousand hours (eight hours a day, five days a week, fifty weeks per year, with two weeks' vacation) to succeed in any area of life. People ask how they can set effective goals. There are multiple methods you can use. I recommend that you start by writing up a list of things you really want in your life, and from there, you can start working toward those things. Once you are in progress with achievement of your goals, you can measure your success based on the type of goal you have. The goal must be refined until it is achieved.

Goals are driven by human philosophy. Different people have different life philosophies. A life philosophy is one of many determining factors that helps you to understand how your life works out in reality. It uses your mind to create and process ideas. After a lot of hard work and dedication, you will have success as an end result to celebrate.

Part of long-term goals is developing personal and pro-fessional growth and progress. Goals also give you the op-portunity to learn more about yourself. Goals help you to become more skillful, more decisive, and a better student. Many people work hard at their jobs, but they forget to work hard at self-improvement. As a result, they have trouble find-ing better opportunities in their lives. When there is no growth or progress, your life will never advance to the next level. You will keep doing the same things that you have always done.

Short-term goals can also be defined as immediate goals. In my opinion, they are designed for tomorrow, next week, next month, or this year. I would consider a goal set for a year from now to be a short-term goal. Personally, I use SMART goals for my short-term goals. SMART stands for Specific, Measurable, Achievable/Attainable, Realistic, Timely. Let's do a deep dive into how the SMART goals work in real life.

Specific: This means that your goal must be well defined, very clear and precise. It must not be ambiguous or confus-ing. You must know exactly what you want to accomplish, and all the details of getting there. For example, you want to learn the Nepalese language in three months. First, you need to make a list of resources that will allow you to learn Nepalese in three months.

Measurable: This means you will need to know how to measure your progress to achieve your goal within the given time frame. You will need to ask yourself whether there is a way to quantify your progress. The answer is yes. In order to do that, you will need to define specific criteria for measuring progress—for example, learning to write the Nepalese alpha-bet in a week. This goal needs to be reviewed and revised as necessary, and your progress measured on a daily basis.

Achievable/Attainable: The goals you set must be

something you can achieve. You know your specific goals and have already measured them, using some criteria. In order to achieve the most ambitious goals, you will need to stretch a bit. In my own experience working with American Peace Corps volunteers in Nepal, they have been able to learn basic Nepalese in three months.

Realistic: How realistic is the goal you have set? Asking yourself this question will cause you to ask whether your goals are within your reach. Then you must ask yourself if you can really commit to the goals. Almost any goal can be realistic when you believe that it can be accomplished and you start working on it. Your goals must be consistent with other goals established, and it must fit with your immediate and long-term plans. In our example, learning Nepalese in three months is realistic, because thousands of people have done so without having any prior language experience other than one mother tongue.

Timely: This means you must set a deadline for your goals. If there is no deadline, then you do not know when you can achieve your goals. Goals must have a clearly defined time frame, including a start date and a target completion date. If you don't have a time limit, then there is no urgency to start taking action toward achievement. In our example, if we don't have a deadline to learn Nepalese in three months, we may not achieve that goal.

Develop the Art of Listening

AS THE TITLE of this section reminds us, listening is an art. We are not taught this at home, school, college, or work. People often ask me what the art of listening really is. I say the art of listening is finding out what the speaker thinks and says about someone or something. There is no question that everyone thinks they are good listeners, even though they are distracted by TV, phone, and human conversations. The art of listening requires people to be positive, patient, open- and clear-minded, non-judgmental, and not to interrupt when the speaker is talking.

Another suggestion I would give is to pay undivided attention to what the speaker is trying to convey. When we are distracted or we do not pay full attention to what the speaker is saying, we might miss the core value of what they are trying to say. This happens often in our personal and professional lives. In my own experience, being a good listener has helped me in building great personal and professional relationships with others. In addition to that, being a good listener helps people to understand each other better, helps to solve difficult issues and problems, resolves conflict, and improves the accuracy of information. This all leads to fewer mistakes and less wasted time.

Let's look at the art of listening from a different perspective. We often try not to listen to 100% of what the speaker has to say, but we must listen without jumping to conclusions. We need to remember that the speaker is using language to represent the thoughts and feelings inside their brain. We don't know what those thoughts and feelings are, and the only way we will find out is by listening carefully.

While listening, we must take in the words and try to envision what the speaker is saying. When the speaker pauses, that is the time to ask clarifying questions. Remember to ask questions only to ensure correct understanding, not to interrupt or impose your agenda. You want to feel what the speaker is feeling, as much as possible.

Sometimes, we need to pay attention to what remains unsaid, and learn to understand nonverbal gestures. When listening, remember that words convey only a fraction of the message, but when we are with people in person, we can feel and detect enthusiasm, boredom, and irritation very quickly by paying attention to facial expressions and body language.

In the end, good listening skills are very important for everyone, because being a good listener allows us to demonstrate and confirm that we are giving our full attention to what the speaker has to say. Being a good listener will help anyone to build good personal and professional relationships, but it also helps to establish communication that will bring harmony to a partnership between two or more people.

Develop A POSITIVE Attitude

ATTITUDE PLAYS A key role in identifying our behavior to others. Dictionary.com defines attitude as "manner, disposition, feeling, position, etc. with regard to a person or thing, tendency or orientation, especially of the mind: a negative attitude, group attitudes." Attitude, in psychology, means a set of emotional behaviors and beliefs toward a particular person or thing. A positive attitude uplifts anyone when they are down and motivates when they are already engaged in something else.

A positive attitude is a mindset that helps people to see and recognize opportunities even in difficult situations. For that reason, people with a positive attitude are cooperative, constructive, optimistic, and enthusiastic about achieving anything in their lives. To put it simply, a positive attitude means positive thinking. In contrast, a negative attitude is a mindset, feeling, or way of being that makes people feel pessimistic, uncooperative, and non-constructive.

In your life, you will meet people with many different attitudes. You just need to teach or train yourself how to deal with them.

There are different ways to improve and keep our attitudes in check as a daily practice:

- Start every morning with a strong and positive attitude.
- Practice meditation to develop patience.
- Avoid cynical and negative people.
- Have fun and cultivate a sense of humor.

- Take breaks between tasks.
- Create a gratitude journal.
- Take action with purpose but let go of expectations.
- Make a habit of forgiving the limitations of others.
- Do not compare yourself to others.
- Always express gratitude—say "thank you" and "please."
- Always expect the best out of every situation instead of the worst.
- Always spend more time with those who share your positive attitude.
- Be kind and positive even when things look difficult to handle.

Sometimes people ask me how to show their positive attitude. There are many ways to do it, but here is a list of things that I recommend:

- When meeting someone, shake hands firmly, make good eye contact, listen carefully to understand what is being conveyed by the speaker, pay attention to the topic being discussed, smile often, and appreciate the time being spent with you.
- Demonstrate who you are with physical and verbal expression.
- While talking, be confident and stay positive.
- Even if it's a tough situation, lighten up the mood by smiling when appropriate, depending on the situation.
- While talking, never complain about or criticize other people or circumstances.
- Do not disagree with the speaker after listening to them, even if you do not agree.

I'd like to share an example of how people with a good attitude can have a disproportionate impact on someone's life. I
am sure many of you have been in this situation. I am talking
about someone who wins your heart by demonstrating a good
work ethic and attitude, and a positive philosophy, honesty,
integrity, and hard work. Being with someone like that makes
you feel that you rarely find such a person to help you in your
personal and professional life. You do not think twice about
supporting them when they need help. You cannot imagine
that such a beautiful person could ever be anything other than
good.

I learned that lesson from a friend of mine who was in
charge of helping a family member to remodel a small com-
mercial building. He met a very nice contractor—a great guy
with a good attitude. They met and talked about the project.
They worked hard together to get the project done. Over the
course of a year, they learned a lot about each other, and the
contractor was very loyal to my friend, and vice versa. They
talked a lot about their stories and experiences. The contractor even introduced his brother to my friend. He was a very
nice person who made my friend feel that he was one of the
best people he had ever met in his life. Whenever my friend
would communicate with him, he would say, "Yes, sir—I am
on top of everything." My friend blindly trusted this person
from the bottom of his heart. The contractor was paid on time,
and the two of them communicated openly and agreed on
everything, to make sure they were on the same page.

One day, the contractor did not show up. The subcontrac-
tor, who had come to install a door, waited for hours to have
him come and clarify something that only he could explain.
He did not respond to phone calls, messages, or emails. He
was the one who had set up the date and time for the door

installation, and then he didn't show up. It was two days after Christmas, and the whole situation was a disaster. I told my friend, "Let it go, and move forward." He took my advice and let it go, but he contacted the contractor by phone call, text message, and email because he had the keys to the building, as well—but he never responded. My friend hired another contractor and finally got the project done. Now, we heard that he was working somewhere else. He betrayed our trust and became irresponsible. Only God knew what made him change from being good to evil, while demonstrating such impractical behavior and deceiving people who had hired him. As a human, we still wish him the best.

We learned a good lesson. It doesn't take long to change someone's mind and attitude. The moral of the story is that it's hard to believe that someone can change, after you've trusted them with good reason. It also teaches us never to trust someone in a short period of time, because immediate empathy and attraction can make us blind. That person could be anyone in your life. You just need to train yourself how to handle these kinds of situations. People are responsible when they volunteer to complete tasks. That is called maturity. I would recommend engaging a legal advisor before hiring a contractor, as there are unprofessional people who have attitude problems about money and who won't get the job done. Finally, it all begins with you and your attitude, and how you project your attitude to others. When people do not communicate well and stop taking responsibility for their actions, we can do nothing about it.

Establish Daily Self-Discipline

A KEY TO success in any area of your life is strict self-discipline on a daily basis. This is one of the challenges for all of us in our daily lives. There is nothing more important than taking good care of your mental and physical health as a top priority. It is something you must do for yourself—no one can do it for you or on your behalf. If you are strong enough mentally and physically, you can help others to develop their mental and physical health as well. After that, you can attain self-discipline in other areas of life—financial, social, intellectual, and spiritual. You may not always have the exact outcome you want, but self-discipline will still play a major role. No matter what area of life you want to succeed in, you must demand self-discipline. That is a mantra for success.

Self discipline involves enthusiasm, high self-esteem, self-reliance, self-confidence, and a positive attitude. It teaches us how to handle our daily "must-do" action items. "Must" means "required." That is a sign of success in any field. "Must do" means must do and there are no excuses. People wait for good things to start later or today or tomorrow or next week or next month or this year. I say start now. There will never be a "perfect time" to start a project. It is not always easy, but it is doable and can be done. Reaching your goal also requires good practice, consistency, and patience. As a formal martial artist, I learned that if I practiced any technique in an incorrect way, I would only reinforce my errors. What I mean is that your practice does not discern the difference between correct and incorrect form, so you may need a mentor, coach, teacher, or instructor to make sure you're not reinforcing bad habits.

With all of the above being said, I would recommend you make the most of your morning, and I recommend the following activities. These kinds of well-disciplined daily habits will make you feel strong in your mental and physical health. As a result, you will feel more energetic, happy, healthy, peaceful, and more fulfilled.

a. When you wake up in the morning, your brain might be dehydrated. Ideally, you should drink a minimum of two to four glasses of warm water. Not only does this help to hydrate your brain; it also helps to cleanse your digestive system. According to Ayurvedic principles, it is recommended that you take a quick cold shower—as cold as you can tolerate. This will help to boost your immune system. This is not medical advice and may not be appropriate for people with certain medical conditions. I am sharing this based on experiences that were helpful to me. Please consult with your doctor before trying any of these suggestions.

b. Meditation helps to improve your emotional health. We all are not the same individuals and we do not see the same things in the same way, no matter what we are doing in our lives. Each of us is unique on this planet. You may not like or enjoy meditation, but I recommend that you do some research about it before making your decision. That will allow you to decide whether meditation will benefit you. I can tell you from experience that if you have not meditated before, you will need to learn patience. It might not be easy right away, but it will be very beneficial. Try for 15-20 minutes at least twice a day—in the morning and in the afternoon. The benefits of meditation have been well documented, including stress and anxiety relief, more clarity, and more self-control.

My secret to leading a happy, peaceful, and successful life is that I made the decision to go to Maharishi University of Management in Fairfield, IA in 1999, where I learned Transcendental Meditation—TM—and got my second master's degree, in management and information technology. The TM technique is very simple, easy, natural, effortless, effective, and fun. It takes 15-20 minutes twice a day. Practicing this technique gives energy, enjoyment, peace, happiness, rest, and self-actualization. I want to mention that the TM program is not a diet, a lifestyle, or a religion. It does not require concentration or contemplation, and it is not difficult. I have been practicing Transcendental Meditation for several decades. I would strongly recommend visiting www.mum.edu for more details.

A selection from "The Transcendental Meditation – TM Book – How to enjoy the rest of your life by Denise Denniston and Peter McWilliams – illustrated by Barry Geller:

The Transcendental Meditation (or TM) techniques was introduced to the United States by Maharishi Mahesh Yogi in 1959. People started the TM techniques, liked it, and told their friends, who started and in turn told their friends, who then also started. Students especially appreciated the value of Maharishi's message; "Man is born to enjoy, to create, and to radiate happiness." By the end of the 1960's, hundreds of thousands of people were practicing the TM technique. The reason most of these people began is because their friends had recommended it.

Then, in 1970, Dr. Robert Keith Wallace of the U.S. began scientific research into the effects of the Transcendental Meditation technique on the mind and body. In his first set of experiments he discovered that during the TM technique, the metabolic rate is reduced by 16% in a matter of minutes. During sleep the metabolic rate is usually reduced by only 12% over a period of many hours. This means that the TM technique quickly provides a state of rest that is much deeper than sleep. These findings were made even more remarkable by the fact that the mind remains alert and awake during this rest – that there is no loss of consciousness as there is during sleep. Dr. Wallace called this unique state of mind and body functioning "restful alertness."

Scientists throughout the world over began studying the effects of the TM technique. The results of these studies, printed in dozens of scientific journals and reported in hundreds of newspapers and magazines, have been responsible for the increasing interest in the TM program over the past few years. These scientific studies offer a vision of man with greater clarity of mind, improved health, and freedom from tension, anxiety, stress. The Transcendental Meditation program changes the quality of life from poverty, emptiness, and suffering to abundance, fulfillment, and happiness.

c. Breathing exercises: In general, breathing exercises will help control your mind. There are many types of breathing exercises. Deep breathing is considered to be one of the best ways to lower stress in the body. When you breathe deeply, it sends a message to your brain to calm down and relax. Just spending a few minutes each day practicing deep breathing can easily decrease stress and anxiety, as well as help you to relax your mind and body, and improve your sleep quality. Anyone can practice a simple abdominal breathing exercise for relaxation. Inhale slowly and deeply through your nose. Keep your shoulders relaxed. Repeat several times. As you breathe in, say to yourself, "I am mentally free and physically relaxed." You can also focus attention on your breathing during Asana, if you practice yoga. First inhale through your nose, then open your mouth and exhale slowly, making a "ha" sound. You may want to try it a few times, and then close your mouth, keeping the back of your mouth positioned in the same way you did to make the "ha" sound as you exhale through your nose.

It is very important to breathe correctly for overall health. Please consult with experts before practicing this technique. Below are some benefits of correct breathing:

- relaxes mind and body
- lowers stress
- lowers blood pressure
- detoxifies the body
- reduces inflammation
- improves digestion
- improves posture
- increases energy level

This exercise is worth considering, but you may want to ask yourself what your end goal is. Again, none of the recommendations in this book are medical advice, and you should ask your doctor before starting any new practice.

d. Physical exercise: Not only will physical exercise help you to create the body you want, it will also help you to be active throughout the day. Remember to add this element to your daily morning routine. Physical exercise may be jogging, swimming, dancing, cycling, walking, gardening, etc., all of which are considered to be aerobic exercise. You can choose from many different activities. Physical exercise has been proven to reduce anxiety and depression. It also improves mental health by lifting negative moods and improving self-esteem and cognitive function. It's a good idea to have a regular aerobic exercise routine that gets you to an optimal heart rate and makes you sweat. Regular exercise has many benefits, including: feeling happier, feeling more energetic and stronger, losing weight, strengthening muscles and bones, stabilizing energy levels, reducing the risk of chronic disease/illness, improving skin quality, improving brain health and memory, feeling more relaxed, and getting better sleep. Your day will depend on how you start it. Not everyone is the same. So, I am creating segments for each category, to give you ideas about how to make your day better every day.

e. It has been said that food is medicine for the human body. On top of that, eating nutritious food should be your number one priority. You may want to consider the fact that you need to eat nutritious and healthy food as medicine, every day. If not, you will need manufactured medicine, sooner or later. I would recommend that you do some research on a healthy diet on your own, to understand what type of food works best for you to keep your body healthy and energetic all day long, whether you are eating breakfast, lunch, or dinner. Everyone metabolizes food differently. Similarly, the same medication prescribed for multiple people who have the same disease may not affect each of them in the same way. Make a note of the fact that great food in the body equals great fuel to strengthen the immune system. Realize that all the foods we eat are processed through the stomach. So, the stomach must be healthy, as well as having a great immune system. If the stomach goes bad, no matter how hygienic or healthy or nutritious our food is, the stomach cannot process it properly. As a result, disease will pop up, and you will be sick. As you will see, sometimes people just want to fill up their stomachs without caring what they are putting into their bodies. Be careful with what you eat every day. I know we are all busy, but to quote Mahatma Gandhi, "A man will sacrifice his health for wealth, then spend his wealth trying to get back his health." The mantra is to take care of your health first, and integrate self-care with your other tasks.

At the end, it's up to you how you want to handle your daily life. You might want to take into consideration that 90% of your enthusiasm for what you really want to do in your life comes from your inner heart and soul, and 10% will come from your outside environment. Keep in mind that 80% of success in life is psychological and 20% is mechanics. All success comes from how we treat our body and mind through regular diet, exercise, thought processes, whom we talk to on a regular basis and how, what information we gather for self-development, and what we study. That is what you become.

Change What You Can Change, and Accept What You Cannot Change

HUMAN LIFE IS simple, but sometimes people make it very complicated. You can change yourself, but you can't change anyone else on this planet. Your goals in life must be set by you, because it is your life. You have about 35,000 choices to make in all areas of your life, every single day. What is happening in your life today has to do with the choices you have made. Some choices can be influenced by other people. When you try to do something, people can ask what, when, where, how, and why you are doing it. Those things are beyond your control, and you cannot change them. We always want things to go our way, or we feel sad, frustrated, and unhappy. That is the normal human condition. Where there are challenges, there will also be opportunities and difficulties. Every difficulty and challenge also presents an opportunity. The opportunities created by challenges will eventually lead you toward where you want to be or what you want to become.

There are many things in our lives that we say we want to change, but we never take serious action. This means we do not make a commitment, and we do not want to be held accountable and responsible. Sometimes people say, "I cannot change that." In reality, the problem isn't that they cannot change—it is that they do not really want to change. My recommendation is that if you really want to change something in your life but find yourself struggling with obstacles, find ways to overcome them—take a calculated risk, if necessary, and make a realistic change. This will help you to achieve whatever you want to do in your life. Change requires 100% commitment and courage and 100% concentrated effort, emotion, and energy in the right direction at the right time, or else it will remain suspended. When you look at the word "change," if you take away the "c" and the "e," you are left with "hang." That is what happens with most of the people around you—they just hang, not taking action. Don't be like them. They want change but never take any action. They spend time in analysis paralysis rather than actually taking action. They never get anywhere.

Things may not always go as planned, even though the plan has been well reviewed and analyzed by many experienced people in the same field. Let me give you an example. Imagine that you will be driving a car, and you know your destination. The car engine and tires are inspected, the car is filled with gas, and the map or GPS is all set. You know where you will be going. Until you start your car and set out, you won't go anywhere. Up to this point, you have control of everything. There is no guarantee that you will get to your final destination without any difficulties. This is where you must learn to accept unexpected circumstances in life. There might be a few unplanned incidents, such as being stopped by the highway patrol for no apparent reason. Do you have any control over what the highway patrol does? Or you might have to stop driving due to heavy rain, snow, or wind. Can you do anything to influence Mother Nature to behave the way you want her to? There might be an instance in which the car won't start after you get gas. Or what if you have to take a detour due to road construction, which might end up delaying you by an hour or two? We need to prepare in advance in order to make things work for us. Most people do not prepare for unexpected situations. There is no such thing as starting at Point A and going to Point B without following the path or process. Life is not easy or cut and dried. All we can do is change what we can change, and accept what we cannot change. If all of us did this, the world would be a very peaceful place with no significant conflict. We just need to be aware of what can go wrong in our lives and how we can manage and handle those issues in positive ways.

Cultivate Your Self-Esteem and Growth

WHEN WE TALK about self-esteem, that is a quality determined by our achievements and accomplishments, and by what we believe other people think of us. It really deals with how we see, think about, and speak about ourselves and others, and how we treat ourselves and others.

According to the dictionary, the definition of self-esteem is "a realistic respect for or favorable impression of oneself; self-respect." I learned in childhood is that self-esteem is satisfaction and joy in being who we are. It explains what we see and value in ourselves and others. Obviously, when we feel and choose good things for ourselves, that impacts others around us, as well. The way we can build our self-esteem is by making the right choices every day, in positive ways. The average person makes about 35,000 choices every day. On top of that, being consistent in developing a positive attitude of gratitude will strengthen your existing self-esteem.

Most importantly, when you have high self-esteem, you believe in yourself, and that makes you feel appreciated by others. Also, high self-esteem allows you to enjoy who you are, and your accomplishments. Not only can high self-esteem help you develop a "can-do" attitude, it also makes you feel good no matter what you do.

When people have high self-esteem, they always help other people, try new ideas and concepts, and learn from others. They are very clear about the fact that failing in a specific task does not make them a failure for the rest of their lives. These people never allow themselves to quit on things that they really want to achieve. They always go above and beyond towards their goals. They change the plan but not the destination. It is more like taking a detour—meaning that they know exactly where they want to go, but if the planned route has some obstacles, they know they need to take a different route to get there. Eventually, they will arrive. They are pretty clear in their minds and they know that quitters never win. Hence, they establish a persistent habit of not quitting anything once they start, and they take calculated risks. They keep trying until they achieve what they want and become the winner.

I have learned that lack of self-esteem may push people toward wrong and destructive life paths, such as using alcohol and drugs, turning to crime, etc. The real tool to maintain self-esteem is to accept everything about who we are, and love, accept, and respect others for who they are. Complaining about our lives weakens our self-esteem and makes us feel we cannot do anything in our lives, because we are influenced by negative and cynical people around us.

When we are fully motivated and positive, our self-esteem rises, and we begin seeing opportunities in every difficulty. We see good things around us coming from everywhere. Start appreciating what we have been given by Mother Nature, including the Himalayan Mountains, the sun, the moon, the sky, the sea, the oceans, etc. People with high self-esteem strongly believe in and learn to enjoy everyone and everything as they are. For example, we show high self-esteem by speaking respectfully to our parents, family members, teachers, and friends and in the proper tone of voice with correct language.

We can always increase our self-esteem by sharing valuable knowledge, experience, and expertise with those around us, as appropriate. Another way to increase self-esteem is to love, care about, and support other people unconditionally. When we put love and compassion into action for someone else, that makes us feel great. When we feel great about ourselves, we feel confident in our abilities. We do not speak badly of others, and we do not criticize them. That means we can talk freely and openly to anyone, without problems or issues.

When we communicate with people, it is very important that we speak in a polite tone, with positive language, rather than being rude or aggressive. We can influence our surroundings and make the world a great place to live, being kind to ourselves and others. We need to make sure that we always respect others' privacy and rights when dealing with them. Doing so will tell others who we are, through our awareness and confidence. Self-awareness is being aware of who we are, what we are doing, and what is going on around us at the present moment. We need to value self-awareness with high self-esteem. That kind of behavior makes a huge difference to those who really love and care about you. When we want to feel good about how others treat us, we also want others to feel good about how they are treated by us. In order to encourage those who lack confidence, we should say something like, "You can do it!" or "You can make it!" This can really have a positive effect on their morale.

I have seen many people in the world with high self-esteem. They have built a legacy through their actions, for the next generation and the generations to come. They always look for an opportunity to do something positive and good for others—through their actions, through their contributions, or even by giving someone moral inspiration or a little smile.

It's totally up to us how we want to live our beautiful human life. I often make an international call to Nepal, using a prepaid calling card. It makes me realize that life is like a prepaid calling card. From my point of view, we can use this concept in two ways. One way to look at it is that when the time on the card is used up, it will expire and cannot be used anymore. Another way to look at this is that if the allocated minutes have not all been used but the card itself has expired, it is equally useless. In the same way, our life has its span, and we must accept that fact, whether we want to or not. It is a question of how we want to use our life. How humans use the minutes on the prepaid calling card of their lifespan on earth matters the most. What I mean is that you should always be inspired to try to make a difference in the world!

Most researchers agree that we can influence our self-esteem and that of others. Nathaniel Branden suggests six cornerstones of self-esteem: living consciously, self-acceptance, self-responsibility, self-assertiveness, living purposefully, and personal integrity. In my own personal experience, some fundamental components of self-esteem include inward confidence, a positive attitude with gratitude, faith, hope, caring, love, generosity, and forgiveness.

When we see ourselves as confident, strong, and capable of doing anything mentally and physically, our behavior will automatically reflect what we do for ourselves and others. Positive energy will fully cooperate to take us along with action to where we want to be. Wherever our attention goes toward achieving anything in life, our energy flows along with our focused action, and things will move along the path to success. It is very important that we train ourselves in the areas of our passion. But having passion, by itself, does not take us anywhere unless we also focus on personal growth and on taking appropriate action. Of course, you can find experts to guide you in your areas of interest. I would recommend learning all you can from mentors and experts, either as formal or informational training. The ways you implement what you learn will affect people around you. Your consciousness and awareness, coupled with a positive attitude, will make the garden of your mind nice and clean at all times. No weeds will have a chance to sprout.

When we cultivate a positive attitude and high self-esteem, we begin to see positivity in others, and we see their value and expertise. Our actions show our attitude and behavior to others and are evaluated by others. So, it is important that we treat other people with the highest standards of respect. Respect means being nice and kind to other people, which will eventually help us to grow our self-esteem as well. Having a positive attitude and caring personality will allow us to be accepted by our nearest and dearest loved ones, our family members, coworkers, and community members. Sometimes, society can be a great source of inspiration and can influence people through demonstrating positive attitudes and actions, which gives others an opportunity to grow as well.

The other way we demonstrate how we care for our family and society is through our actions. Many of us do not realize that our community offers opportunities to all of us, to care about and share many life lessons. But remember that you need to study your community before spending too much time in it. Some societies make a big difference in the world with their commitment to change. Some do not care about people and can damage existing relationships with family and friends. It's up to you how you want to get involved with your community. The only person in your community who can change you is yourself. For that matter, it does not matter what society looks like for you—you can always demonstrate a positive attitude and behavior to people around you.

When every community becomes a place to talk about our concerns, then we will have heaven on earth, and we will start to feel that this world is the best place to live and enjoy life. When we are self-aware, we begin to appreciate what we were given by nature, because we see a lot of positive energy coming through the natural beauty surrounding us. I am from Nepal, where we see rivers, the sea, and the Himalayas every day. Each of these natural resources gives us a lot of positive energy. Nature has such power that more than half of human health issues can be cured through spending more time in nature. I would recommend to anyone to go for a walk in nature, ride a bike with friends or family, walk your dog, watch birds, draw something that interests you and sparks your imagination, read something that helps you grow, hike, go for a run, or simply bask in the sun, which provides enough Vitamin D to change your mood. When we believe that we are here because of mother nature and her power, we will see the value of the natural power in us. For example, if trees do not give us oxygen, we cannot survive in this world at all. People like you and me can make this world a better place to live, through our positive thoughts and actions.

As part of self-esteem, each of us must remember humans are unique creatures on this planet, and also that each human being is unique unto itself. Each of us has a special quality that we can give to someone on this planet. When we put the quality of our talent into perspective, we will create more coherence within our family, community, society, country, and the world.

Becoming Attunded to Human Communication

COMMUNICATION IS A good partnership between two or more individuals to keep them on the same page. Great communication can help people to identify where confusion and misunderstandings are. Learning great communication skills requires learning to understand how others perceive and process information. That is one of the hardest parts of effective communication. There are even situations in which communication itself interferes with good communication. It is not always easy to communicate effectively with others.

I will try to illustrate the principle of effective communication with a little story about a man named Tom. He was a very helpful person in the community where he had been serving. Tom was polite, with a soft voice. One day, one of his community members, Ben, reached out to Tom and asked if he would be willing to help someone in Ben's family with the task of hiring someone for a small family business. Ben thought Tom could help. Having that idea in mind, Ben picked up the phone and called Tom. After a quick conversation, Ben wanted to make sure what they discussed was fully understood by Tom.

Ben sent Tom a quick text message: "Hello. It was nice talking to you. Thanks for your time—I appreciated it. Regarding the job we discussed, please have interested parties contact me directly. Applications for this job will be closing soon, and

HR would like to give our internal community members priority before the job is posted elsewhere. They pay the industry standard hourly rate plus benefits."

Tom immediately replied, "Let me forward this to some folks I know. They already have jobs, but let me see. It might take a little time, because I want to talk to them in person, and then I will update you. If I contact them by text message, they might not take it seriously."

The next day, Ben thanked Tom for sending an email on another, unrelated matter. Then Ben asked, via text message, "By the way, did you get a chance to talk to anyone about the job we discussed the other day?"

Tom said, "No—I can talk when we get together. I checked with some people, but they said they already have jobs and are not looking right now." Ben replied, "That's fine."

Tom started asking Ben about wages, etc. via text message. Ben called and discussed the questions with Tom over the phone, as the information was too sensitive to give via text. In the course of their conversation, Tom mentioned that some employers had unfair management and wage practices. They finished their conversation and hung up, as they both were busy. Ben messaged Tom, "They are nice people, and they make everything clear before hiring. So, if someone is unfair to employees, it will not be them. They can't speak for other employers, but they would be more than happy to talk to anyone who wants to work for them." Tom replied that he didn't have any leads. Ben said, "No problem. All you can do is help when possible."

Tom replied, "I can refer only, and if you keep following up frequently, I'll be overselling." Ben said he didn't understand. Tom replied, "If they are interested, they will contact you." Ben agreed. Tom added, "Overselling means you are pressuring me too much. I'm not your employee."

Ben said, "No, of course not. I'm treating you as a community member—that is all."

Tom replied, "You keep calling and texting me the same thing again and again for the past eighteen hours. I always help others, but I have never felt pressure like this."

Ben closed the topic, saying, "All I can say is maybe you have too much going on? Maybe you're having a bad day? I'm really surprised by your behavior. How many times have I actually texted and talked to you on this topic? The way you usually talk in the community meeting isn't reflected in the way you're communicating with me now. Please do not bother responding to this message—this conversation is over. God bless you, and have a great day."

The moral of this story is that we cannot judge a book by its cover. Coming from a management and IT background, I can tell you that making assumptions about someone or something is not an effective way to communicate. Also, you probably noticed that Tom misrepresented what Ben had done, saying he had tried to reach him for the past eighteen hours, which I knew to be incorrect because I was there on both days and witnessed the incident. The behavior exhibited by Tom went on to create more problems in the future with others, as well. Sometimes we see things as good when they are not, and the people we believe to be good aren't always the way we think they are. Another lesson is that we never really know how people feel about us or what they see. It is beyond our control. Humans typically get around twenty-seven emotional expressions every day as part of their behavior and attitudes toward people and situations. It is up to us how we want to feel, and to take responsibility to create our emotions toward situations. We decide whether we want to keep things simple or complicated as a result of a conversation we have with another person.

Effective communication makes a huge difference in our everyday lives. One day, my six-year-old daughter had a high fever, and we had to rush her to the ER at 1:00 a.m. A nurse came to check on her, and then there was no communication after an hour of observation. I called the front desk and let them know I needed immediate help, as my daughter was shaking. There was no response from anyone for another 45 minutes. The nurse finally showed up and apologized for not being able to help promptly. I appreciated how hard they were working with limited staff, but not having adequate support in the emergency department was putting patients' lives at risk.

After the doctor finally checked on my daughter, two ladies came to interview me about my experience. First of all, I appreciated how dedicated they were to helping their patients. I provided constructive feedback, which they made note of, explaining clearly step by step why it was so important always to have someone on standby in the emergency room. Finally, the ladies asked if they could take my comments to their manager. I said yes, that was my intent. They were happy to get my constructive feedback, and they left the room. My point here is that whether we are at home or in the office or anywhere else, we need to communicate well with everyone. That will ensure that all parties are on the same page as far as what, when, where, who, how, and why. Especially in an emergency room, human lives will be at risk if medical attention is not given in a timely manner.

While I was at the ER, the doctor recommended keeping my daughter in the hospital for the next 24 hours. The next day, a family member who was staying with me came to visit us. They said that the water dispenser in the refrigerator was broken. I didn't worry too much about it, as it didn't seem like a priority item. The same night, my wife came to give me a break and said she could take care of the refrigerator. I didn't fully register her comment, as I was thinking about work. She didn't explain that the refrigerator had completely stopped working. Nobody communicated with me clearly enough to explain that a repairman needed to be called right away.

The following morning, we brought our daughter home from the hospital. When we got home, the refrigerator door was open. My family said the refrigerator was broken. I asked why nobody had told me about it. My wife said she had told me, but I might not remember because of everything else that had been going on. Also, when other family members had been talking about the water dispenser being broken, I asked if they had checked the lock system in the refrigerator. I thought it was an issue just with the water dispenser, though it was more extensive than that. However, I didn't know the full extent of the problem until I got home. I should have asked for more details, but I had assumed they would give me the details I needed. We kept our food outside on the porch; the weather was close to freezing, which helped as far as saving the food.

The bottom line is that things like this can happen in any household. In this scenario, if I had understood what was going on earlier, I would probably have moved it into my list of priority items and taken care of the refrigerator issue right away. No one explained clearly what was going on. I just wanted to keep things simple. I called for service, and the issue was resolved. It is very important that we communicate well with one another, regardless of who we are dealing with. Poor communication always results in bigger issues that take more time and effort to resolve.

When we communicate, we must confirm that the

information being conveyed is very clear to the recipient, who needs to know exactly what information is being relayed. Here is another great example of poor communication that I experienced. One day, I was flying to South Carolina, USA, via Charlotte, North Carolina, USA. Since I had about four hours of travel time ahead of me, I thought that I would meet up with my friend, Babu. I called him and we made a plan to meet at the Charlotte airport. I sent him my itinerary and boarding pass before getting on the plane at Minneapolis, Minnesota.

Babu said that he would head out to the airport straight from his office. I said fine. We were excited to see each other again after a long time. Upon arrival at the airport, I called Babu and said that I had just landed. Babu asked me if I were at Terminal One. I said I was. He asked me to come to Gate Five. I said there was no Gate Five—just Gate Four. I asked him to come to Door D. He said there was no Door D. After talking on the phone for about 30 minutes, walking from gate to gate, Babu asked if I were at the Raleigh airport, and I said no, I was at the Charlotte airport. He didn't realize that's where I was. I asked if he had checked the boarding pass and itinerary I provided. He said no—he just assumed I would be at Raleigh. We both had a good laugh.

Babu learned a good lesson—he should have carefully checked the information I provided him, before going to the airport. This is a great example of why clear communication is important. If Babu had carefully reviewed the itinerary and boarding pass prior to driving to the airport, he would not have gone to the wrong location. He wasted his time and effort, and we were not able to see each other.

Embrace Diversity and Inclusion

EMBRACING DIVERSITY AND inclusion is one of the biggest keys to personal and professional growth. Even though there are indefinite differences between people, diversity and inclusion are critical elements of human life. Humanity encompasses a group of unique individuals from the globe who acquaint and integrate with each other in community and society.

Diversity refers to the traits and characteristics that make people unique due to gender, race, age, nationality, culture, etc., while inclusion refers to the behaviors and social norms that ensure people feel welcome and comfortable being around other people in their community and society. A philosophy of inclusion is a way of thinking and acting that allows every individual to feel accepted, valued, significant, safe, and secure. Not only is inclusion crucial for diversity efforts to succeed, but also, an inclusive culture will prove beneficial for staff engagement and increased productivity in any organization.

In our day-to-day life, we work with people who are different from us in many ways. Understanding the value of diversity and inclusion will help us to feel comfortable and secure in working with other people. I learned diversity and inclusion concepts when I was with the American Peace Corps/Nepal in 1993. Respecting diversity helps dispel negative stereotypes and personal biases about different individuals. We used to teach cultural adaptation strategy to the American Peace

Corps volunteers in Nepal. Our cultural diversity helped us to recognize and respect "ways of being" that are not necessarily our own. Because of this, we interacted with other workers and the American Peace Corps volunteers and built bridges to trust, respect, and understanding of cross-cultural values between the United States of American and Nepal.

Inclusion mattered to us because we knew that it would be harmful for our project team to leave out a person or a group or make them feel like they did not belong. It would hurt the person excluded and it would hinder the group that would exclude them, because then they could not learn from that person's insights, experiences, or perspective. There are a lot of benefits to inclusion. The first, biggest benefit of inclusion is that it builds good friendships. This will help increase social interactions, relationships, and networks. This is one of the biggest factors of inclusion that we can apply to daily life.

Inclusion is very important for everyone, because we would like other people to feel that their nationality, culture, values, and experience are respected. We all want to be treated with respect for our nationality, culture, and values, so we need to respect others' nationality, culture, and values as well. This allows everyone to learn from each other about their nationality, culture, values, and experiences.

In a nutshell, diversity and inclusion play a vital role in society to change the perspective and perception of human behavior to treat everyone with love and respect. Not only does a philosophy of inclusion encourage community or society to value, accept, and nurture each person, but it also can help develop the social, financial, economic, and spiritual life of the community, society, country, and the whole world.

Respect Yourself and Others

RESPECT FOR OTHERS is just as important as self-respect. For example, if you are outside and you greet someone, 99.9% of the time, you will get a response. A lot can happen, depending on where you go after your morning routine. No matter where you will be and what you will be doing, it all begins with you. A majority of individuals at work might be dealing with peers, coworkers, managers, or senior management officials, depending on their role at work. Business managers will be dealing with employees, landlords, tenants, customers, and vendors. Do not expect everything to go to plan or make decisions based on whether you are merely an employee, or the owner. The first thing to keep in mind is to let the environment work for you. Many times, people go against their environment, which creates a lot of problems no matter where you are and regardless of the situation. It all begins with how you see things, how you perceive the world, and how you take action to address issues or concerns.

When we meet people, it is always nice to smile and initiate communication. A smile will automatically make a person feel friendly and respected. In the end, complicated issues can be resolved smoothly and peacefully. People can even feel respect in how you speak to them over the phone. Each case is unique, so each case should be addressed separately, depending on the needs of the situation. It takes time and courage to develop the determination to create a positive environment no matter where you go. My recommendation for everyone is to change what you can change, and accept what you cannot change.

I would like to share a story from my life when I lived in West Des Moines, Iowa. I saw a man in his mid-fifties with his twelve-year-old son at the park. They were both practicing with a soccer ball. A man passing by gave a big smile to the man, who stopped and introduced himself as John. They shook hands, and the newcomer introduced himself as Kevin. John and Kevin briefly talked about a few topics—life, family, relationships, work, society, etc. Kevin revealed that he had a negative mindset. He was a software engineer who had recently moved to West Des Moines from Seattle. After a few minutes of conversation, Kevin asked, "By the way, what are people like in this neighborhood?" John asked what the people had been like where Kevin used to live. Kevin replied that they were pretty bad, and he hadn't liked his neighborhood. John said, "Hmmm. People are pretty bad here, as well. Too bad—so sad." Kevin thanked him and left the park. John and his son played soccer a little longer, and then went back home.

A few days later, John and his son came to practice soccer in the same park. This time, John and his son met another man who had brought his small children to play soccer as well. John smiled at the newcomer and introduced himself. The newcomer introduced himself as Calvin.

John said, "You look like you're new to the area." Calvin replied that he was moving from Chicago to take a job as a project manager, and he asked John what he did.

"I am a Certified Life Coach, and I help people to get motivated about their lives and help them grow."

Calvin said, "Great to know. I should come to you sometime when I feel down." They both laughed, and then went on to chat about various topics. Before Calvin left, he said, "By the way, what are the people like in this neighborhood?" John asked how the people were in Calvin's old neighborhood. "I have a great community in Chicago, and I'm sure it will be the same here," Calvin said. John agreed that the neighborhood was great, and the people were nice and friendly. John's son Nick was listening to his dad and remembered that just the other day, he'd said the neighborhood was unfriendly. The boy was confused but didn't say anything to his dad while they were at the park. After they came home, they both took a shower and sat down with the rest of the family for dinner.

Nick said, "Dad, the other day when we met a stranger in the park, you told him we had an unfriendly neighborhood, but today you said to someone else that we have a good and friendly neighborhood. I don't understand, and I'm confused."

John had a big smile on his face. He said, "You see, son, what you experience in life depends upon how you see the world around you. If you treat people well, they will treat you well. Of course, there are exceptions, but that's a general rule. There is nothing you can do to change others. The man to whom I said our community was bad was a negative person. When we were talking, I felt and heard negativity in his mind and thought processes. We talked a lot about his software development career, his family, and his community. He didn't seem to be cooperative when he described how he had dealt with his coworker who needed help with a task. He also explained how he treated someone in his community badly due to an unintentional error they had made. All the actions he performed, and the results he had, were not positive or impressive. I figured that he could have acted differently at work and in his community. It sounded like the issues were within him, but he kept putting the blame on others. So, people in his community were not supportive of him because he did not support and respect others. He did not value them as good citizens and community members. He believed those people were bad, and he will feel the same way when he moves to our community.

"I talked for a while with the man today, as well. When I started talking to him, he shared a lot about his experiences dealing with negative, difficult people who have challenging attitudes. But what I found fascinating was that he was able to establish great relationships with all kinds of people. Plus, he gave me a specific example of a time when someone said something pretty bad about him. He put a positive spin on the situation and had a face-to-face meeting with the person to clarify the situation and resolve it. Eventually, the man with a bad attitude improved his behavior, and they are now good friends. Knowing that, I said we have a great community, because he interacts well with people and he is likely to have a good experience here, as well. The way he looks at things is different from the other man we talked to." This was a valuable life lesson for Nick.

As I stated above, we just need to accept what is happening, in situations where we have no control. If there is something that needs to change and you can change it, then you change. Otherwise, you must accept what you cannot change. Just realize that the most important things in life aren't about being rich or poor, or more or less intelligent. It is important to learn how someone treats another person. It does not matter how long someone lives as much as it matters *how* they live. Respect is not something you learn from someone. It is something you do. If you want to be respected, then learn how to respect others. That is how you get respect from others. Nothing in life happens by itself—every action needs a good plan to be successful.

No matter how much you have learned, it won't do you any good unless you experiment with putting your learning into practice. For example, if we buy food and never consume it, then we have no experience of eating the food. If we consume the food, we will find out how much energy it gives us and whether we like the taste and texture of it. Whatever we learn in life, we need to experiment with it in real life to know how it really works. Then it becomes actual knowledge. If we are suffering, we do so due to lack of knowledge, or due to confusion. For example, if a private pilot takes you up in a plane and during the course of your conversation he says that he wants to give you the plane and jump out with a parachute, you can take the plane, but you won't know how to fly it, even if you've watched him do it. It's not what you've learned in life that matters—it's experience that really counts. Otherwise, your life will be like watching a movie or listening to music—you will tend to forget about it once it is over.

When you are dealing with people, the first thing you notice is your thoughts. Then, your thoughts become feelings. Based on those feelings, we may show emotion to other people—smiling, crying, yelling, raging, etc. The person you are dealing with will start to notice your emotions. Someone might even ask you not to be aggravated because they are only doing their job. In most cases, we become irritated due to lack of knowledge, but in some cases, people are intentionally asking or explaining things that are unnecessary. Once your feeling gets transformed into expressed emotion, it becomes energy, and it becomes magnetic. For example, if you start thinking something positive about what you are doing, you start to imagine positive actions and you get going. Eventually, your positive thoughts are transformed into emotion. The emotion becomes energy and is attached to your positive action. Similarly, if you tend to put your energy into negative emotions, then negative actions will be the result.

When you are having a conversation with someone, it is best to listen more than talk. You need to carefully consider when it is best to listen, and when it is appropriate to speak. If you don't know how to gauge those dynamics, you can study and research the topic. I guarantee you that there is a lot of information available. I am a leader in the information technology industry, but I don't necessarily know everything about every aspect of my job. However, I can train myself on the specific knowledge I need in order to do my job. If I really want to be an expert, then I must study. There is a saying that being is doing and becoming. We become what we do and practice the most. If we want to be happy, then we learn about happiness; to study wealth is to become wealthy. I am talking here about a generic way to handle yourself with people. Each case is unique and must be handled individually. In order to do that, you must understand the skill set you need to deal with any specific individual or organization that you deal with on a daily basis. The best way to deal with people is to value who they are and treat them with love, respect, and positive actions, whether you are working with an individual, an organization, or a business. Communication is really a partnership, regardless of whether it is personal or professional. Ask yourself this: How many times do we fail to ask the right questions at the beginning of a conversation, and how many times do we neglect to ask the appropriate questions at the beginning of a project or plan? Later, people start blaming each other. The blame game must be something you do not play. If you ask yourself why something is happening, you will find the answer to that question. No matter what happens in your life, there is always a 50/50 chance that you will be involved in it.

One thing I want people to understand is that we all have positive and negative experiences when dealing with people. If you really want to be successful, you must learn from both the positive and negative experiences. Positive experiences will teach anyone what to do and how to do it, to succeed; negative experiences teach us what not to do, and how not to do things. As we experience both the positive and negative parts of life, we may not realize that it is human nature to experience both positive and negative thoughts. The important thing to understand is that the positive aspects of life should be dominant and greater than the negative. For example, if your thoughts are 50% positive and 50% negative, you are neutral.

Let's say you have 51% positive and 49% negative thoughts. That means you are right on the border of being a positive-minded individual. If you have 51% negative and 49% positive thoughts, then you are slowly becoming negative-minded. It takes a lot of practice to become a fully positive-minded individual. Negativity is one of the factors that push people into depression and anxiety disorders later in their lives. Based on my own experience, I would not recommend that anyone stay angry for more than five minutes. The best way to handle your anger is to stay away from such scenarios as much as you can. Before the advent of modern technology, when we were angry or mad, we weren't able to communicate immediately with the person we were mad at, because we didn't have smartphones, instant messages, texting, email, etc. After a certain period of time, your temper tends to cool naturally, at which point, people tend to forgive more easily.

Modern technology has revolutionized human communication. There seems to be a lack of discipline and understanding as far as how best to use it. People have cyber fights using chat and on Facebook, Instagram, etc. People instantly communicate without thinking first. For these reasons, many people are fired, get divorced, break up with loved ones, etc. It happens because people have no patience to pause, think, and respond. Sometimes people do not care no matter what you do, whereas other people will not stop loving or caring for you no matter what you do. However, it all begins with you. You are treated in the same way that you treat others. Do not get me wrong—there are many people who never try to understand what "respect" is. It is something they do, but it is not what they know.

Many people do not realize that every human has value. You might be wondering how that can be true. Human value does not come from a wealthy family background, or from exceptional intelligence or worldly success. Let's consider the example of a child lost in a crowd. When that happens, the parent reports to the authorities, and an effort is made to find the child. Nobody will ask what the child's family background is or whether the child is worthy of being found. No matter what the child's race or religion is, the search goes on until it is completed. From that perspective, no human is more important than another. Make sure you know your own value, but also value other people and create a coherent environment to lead a peaceful, responsible, and happy life.

I met a man at the store who introduced himself to me as a truck driver. He wasn't very excited about this job, though he made a living at it. I introduced myself as a Certified Life Coach, Motivational Speaker, and IT professional. I told him he was as important as anyone else on this planet. He asked me to explain. I said, "If a doctor makes a mistake, he may end up taking the life of one person. If you make a mistake, you could take many people's lives." He thanked me and said it had never occurred to him that he is important, too. He shook hands with me and thanked me for what I had said, and he left with a big smile on his face. The key to being a decent person is to respect everyone. You must develop an attitude of unconditional love toward all of humankind, which will help to create a positive, prosperous, and peaceful lifestyle. Love is a natural, emotional, unconditional silent language that only your heart can hear, speak, and explain and only your soul can understand, feel, and realize. There is a big difference between how long we live, and how we live. We need to understand how to live peacefully, happily, and healthfully.

Manage Stress Every Day

BEFORE WE TALK about how to manage stress every day, it is very important to know what stress is. Stress can also be called tension. It can be either internal (illness or disability) or external (family, community, and social environment). It is the human body's reaction to any change that requires alignment, adjustment, or response that exceeds the personal and social resources the individual is able to mobilize. The body typically reacts to these changes with emotional, mental, and then physical responses. Our thoughts create feelings. The feelings create emotions. Emotions are magnetic and interact with the five basic senses of the human body–sight, hearing, smell, taste, and touch. Needless to say, stress is part of human life.

We experience stress when things are not being done the way we expect, or things don't turn out the way they should. Some things that cause stress include being frustrated, fearful, sad, angry, grieved, unhappy, anxious, jealous, regretful, ashamed, overloaded, working to a deadline, worry, and self-criticizing/self-loathing. Stress can come from many sources, including personal health, family, work, and society. Stress can be categorized as physical (health issues), emotional/psychological (frustration, fear, sadness, anger, grief, unhappiness), psychosocial (family relationships, marriage difficulties, home foreclosure, loss of loved ones, etc.), and spiritual (limiting beliefs that do not allow you to succeed).

As you may have heard before, depression, anxiety, and panic attacks are not really signs of weakness leading to an unhealthy life. Rather, they are considered signs or symptoms of remaining strong and rigid for too long under pressure. Ninety-five percent of human illnesses are caused by stress hormones in the body.

Humans manage stress levels starting in childhood, and it is not always easy. The nature of human life is to grow and evolve, and so stress grows as well. It is recommended that we manage stress proactively in order to avoid unexpected mental and physical health issues. From my personal experience, when stress-related feelings, moods, and emotions are pushed into the body, they may create stomach pain, headaches, high blood pressure, fatigue, nausea, anxiety, allergies, and autoimmune syndromes related to ineffective function of the immune system.

One common symptom of stress is negative thoughts. Many people have negative thoughts, but it is up to us how we handle them. Below are a few stress-management tips.

- Develop a positive attitude and be receptive to accepting things that you do not have control over.
- Develop a "don't cry over spilled milk" attitude when things are already done.
- Develop an attitude that failing at something does not mean you are a failure.
- Manage your time wisely every day.
- Smile and laugh often, and make humorous jokes as appropriate.
- Keep a stress diary to jot anything down when it occurs.
- Avoid negative consequences of things not being

done at your best level.
- Be assertive about things instead of being aggressive.
- Practice relaxation techniques such as meditation, breathing exercises, yoga, etc.
- Exercise every day if possible, but at least three times a week.
- Eat a balanced diet on a regular basis.

Emotional stress is a common experience for many people. It is also defined as emotional tension or mental strain. This is not visible through the human body but is expressed through facial and mental expressions by demonstrating certain actions while dealing with others or doing something on their own. Needless to say, too much stress can produce both mental and physical disease. In my own experience, I have seen and learned from many people that signs of emotional stress include anxiety, agitation, changes in personality, compulsive behavior, depression, decline in self-care, irritability, low sex drive/libido, mood swings, and problems with memory and concentration.

It is important that we deal with stress in a timely manner. One of the many things that I recommend people do is not to stay mad for more than five minutes. If we stay in that state too long, we can ruin our whole day. Some people get mad and stay mad all day. That can ruin their whole week. After three months of mental disturbances due to stress, people might start experiencing major mental diseases, such as anxiety disorders. Those who take medication to cure such issues might create diseases a hundred times more destructive in their bodies. It's up to us how we want to manage our daily stress.

Below is a list of few strategies that anyone can use to deal with stress:

- First things first: Be careful about what you eat and drink. Try to eat a well- balanced diet, eating at least three healthy, regular meals a day.
- Always try to see and feel only good things about everyone and everything.
- Get enough sleep—kid and adult sleep hours may vary.
- Exercise regularly—dancing, running, biking, or another aerobic exercise.
- Control your breathing, using breathing exercises. A lot of YouTube videos are available to select from to find what might work best for your body.
- Allocate time for fun, and really take the time to enjoy what you do.
- Work six days of hard work a week and take one day off.
- Read at least one book once a month—it's best if you can read more than one book a month.
- Write in a diary every day—you can also write a letter to your enemy but never send it.
- Often get in touch and get connected with Only Quality People (OQP).
- Often talk with only inspiring people when you're feeling discouraged and low.

Create Happiness and Influence Others

THE BIGGEST CHALLENGE in life is to survive and take good care of yourself. Bringing happiness to your life can be tough, especially if you cannot let your environment work for you and cannot enjoy what you have and what you are surrounded by.

Researchers have found that 85% of US workers do not like their job. They go to work every day and complain about their job. I call that a "slave mentality." Researchers have also found that many people have heart attacks between 8:00 a.m. and 10:00 a.m. on Mondays because it is the beginning of the week and people feel too much stress, depression, frustration, and job insecurity. Often, people say, "I want happiness and peace in my life," but they do not ask themselves what really makes them feel happy and peaceful. Just saying that you want peace and happiness is pretty vague and tough to understand, without knowing what makes you feel happy and peaceful. Once you know what makes you happy and peaceful, then you must take focused action with total commitment in the right direction to make changes. I hear people say they want to improve their English conversational skills, but they never practice with someone who knows how to speak English well.

When I was in high school, I learned the concept of reaping and sowing. It basically says that the mind is like soil, our thoughts are seeds, our actions are water, and our feelings are the sun. Since the mind is like a garden, weeds tend to sprout from time to time. Those are our negative thoughts—thoughts of failure, doubt, and fear. What I recommend to people is that every morning, we get rid of those weeds of negative thoughts by meditating, listening to soothing music, doing yoga, etc. In order for the mind to be beautiful, we need to cultivate it with high self-esteem, happiness, success, kindness, compassion, forgiveness, love, understanding, and gratitude. Human life is constant reaping and sowing. You receive what you give. The energy you put out is what you get back. The mind is fertile ground, and it doesn't care what we plant in it. It will always yield results. It is up to us whether we want to plant fruits of happiness, vegetables of joy, flowers of positive attitude and peace, or weeds of misery and sadness. At the end of the day, you reap what you sow.

There are two factors in our lives that contribute significantly to happiness: internal life and external life. It is important to have a deep understanding of the differences between the two. Our internal life is within ourselves, and nothing affects it except our soul, mind, and individual body. Our external life is affected by the outside world—which could be someone telling you to do something that you agree or disagree with, or someone just acting badly, which makes you feel upset, impacting your internal peace. Let us deep-dive into these two aspects of life that affect our peace, happiness, and good mental and physical health.

Internal Life: From my point of view, your internal life is the most important part of life, where it is necessary to have an inner connection between mind and body, resulting in good mental and physical health. This part of life is also associated with the soul and conscious mind, which are part of mental health. Your consciousness makes you aware, or makes you feel like something is happening. Your internal life has two parts: your *inward internal life* and your *outward internal life*. Your inward internal life is concerned with being calm, creative, positive, loving, caring, accountable, and responsible for yourself. It has to do with mental peace and being free of worry. Your outward internal life has to do with physical health—eating and drinking for optimal health, regular physical exercise, and a nutritious, balanced diet that keeps you energetic and healthy all day.

In my experience, internal life is mind-body coordination. There is no emotional attachment involved. You might want to boost your internal life by practicing internal exercises such as meditation and yoga, as well as physical activities that will help strengthen your mental and physical health, which will allow you to achieve anything you really want in your life. Your internal life has to do with looking within, being with what you have regardless of circumstance. For example, there are many people in the world who have nothing to eat. In contrast, you may be complaining about not being able to find a specific brand of food you are looking for. Some people may not have shoes to wear, and someone else may be complaining about not having a pair of Air Jordans. For me, the internal life is the most important, because it gives inner peace, which is necessary for mental peace. Eventually, mental peace will produce chemicals that help the body to be physically healthy.

Our minds create our thoughts, and our thoughts create our feelings. The feelings we have are transformed into emotion. Emotion becomes energy, and it is magnetic. Energy has no ability to distinguish between the negative and the positive. Whatever we apply our energy toward, our actions will be strengthened, regardless of whether those actions are negative or positive. Likewise, when we put our energy into negative actions, those actions will become powerful. Therefore, before creating any thought, stand guard at the door of the mind to be careful about what is created.

Human pain comes from desire, not action. We need to take action in order to fulfill our desires. When you see change, the desire will go away by itself. We suffer most in life when we have a desire for things to go our way. We do things with desire and conflate that with achievement in our lives. The more we have thoughts and desires, the less we have happiness and joy. It is up to you how you handle your thoughts and desires.

External Life: Our external life is how other people think about us and how we are impacted or influenced by other people. As humans, we have both self-recognition and relationships with family, community, and in society.

There are two parts to our external life as well—the *inward external life*, and the *outward external life*. The inward external life is the life we share with our family. I'm sure you've heard sayings such as: "Having a place to go means you have a home. Having someone to love means you have a family. Having both is a blessing." A combination of home and family is the greatest blessing. The question is how to create a peaceful environment within our family. In my opinion, it starts with the three R's. I started teaching these to my kids when they were five years old. The first R stands for Respect Yourself. The second R stands for Respect Others. The third R stands for taking Responsibility for your actions. When people do not take responsibility for their actions, it means they are immature and cannot function appropriately in society. When the three Rs come together, a good environment is created. Family discord is one of the growing issues in the world, and it happens due to a lack of understanding of family values, and losing the three fundamental Rs. Family stands for "Father and Mother, I Love You." One family member cannot change the reality of the others until they change their mentality and attitude. Family responsibility is a shared responsibility, but individual accountability to develop a positive attitude of gratitude can bring coherence, peace, and happiness into their lives.

Your outward external life has to do with how you are affected by the behavior of other people, and vice versa. When things cannot be accepted as they come, stress is out there, and it will tend to overshadow the happy moments. Just wearing a nice dress does not make you feel young, if you are already old. Wearing make-up will not make you feel beautiful, if you do not already feel beautiful inside. Hiding the natural shape of your body will not make any difference to you, but it will make you look different to others. Your life is all about you. Whether you accept your life or not, it will remain the same until you change your actions to improve your personal growth and positive thought process. Many people in our community and in society want changes, but they continue to do the same things while expecting different results.

We know that people go out and see how others are doing in their lives. Some are envious, whereas others become motivated by the progress of others. Envy is another human disease that you want to avoid. If it does not act as a motivator, it will mutate into a serious psychological disorder. Envy will eventually create negative thoughts, depression, anxiety, and panic attacks. Please note that, as I mentioned earlier, panic attacks are not a sign of weakness. They are a symptom of having remained very strong and silent for too long. The bottom line is that your external life should not ruin your internal life, which will end up taking your happy moments. Instead of being envious, you can take the initiative to do creative work on your life, and grow in that way. Josh Kaufman, the author of *The First 20 Hours: How to Learn Anything...Fast!* claims that you can learn any skill in 20 hours. However, *Outliers* by Malcom Gladwell estimates that it takes about 10,000 hours to become successful at anything.

Change Your Reality By Changing Your Mentality

UNTIL WE CHANGE our mentality, our reality will never change. Our lives feel stagnant because we have been clinging for a long time to the same mentality no matter what we do, where we go, or when, how, and why we do things. It is how people have programmed their mindset. In order to see changes, you must change your mindset and do things differently. Changing your habits will help you to feel more productive, efficient, and effective in your life, and you will positively impact others.

When you are happy, then happy things will happen. Life never changes through luck, hope, or dreams. It will change only when you take different action. Life is like the seasons—spring, summer, fall, and winter. The seasons change naturally, but you have to change within yourself to adjust with them or take advantage of them. Spring runs from March 1 to May 31. Summer runs from June 1 to August 31. Fall runs from September 1 to November 30. Winter runs from December 1 to February 28.

Each season has different lessons to teach. Spring teaches us that opportunities always await us. We need to keep in mind that opportunities follow difficulties, and vice versa. It is like a cycle of seasons. Whenever there is an opportunity, there will also be a difficulty. Spring is followed by winter. Summer teaches us to protect the crops. It is necessary to take care of what you started in the spring. You might have planted the garden, but you will need to get rid of weeds and control bugs in order to keep your garden looking beautiful. In the same way, the garden of our mind needs us to pull weeds every day. It will also need frequent nourishment with fertilizer, and other good gardening techniques. Fall teaches us when it is time to harvest. In human life, it teaches us to take full responsibility for life, no matter what happens to us. People demonstrate maturity by taking full responsibility for their own lives.

Speaking of seasons, I have my own experiences to share. Here is one example. I live in Apple Valley, Minnesota, USA. During the winter, I must keep myself warm by putting on warm clothes when I am out. That will allow me to stay warm and healthy without the extreme cold weather affecting my health. If I don't do this, I will not be able to handle the cold weather. When I am inside, I take off my jacket. In the same way, you might not find happy people around you all the time, and things you do may not always be in your favor throughout the year.

In order to deal with time, place, and circumstances, you cannot expect that the things you do will always be in your favor. Instead, you need to change yourself to let the environment work for you. It is true that it isn't always easy to deal with people, but it's up to you how you handle it. I would recommend that first, you need to build high self-esteem, a positive attitude, and kindness within to deal with others. Then you must respect and build a good relationship with them in order to survive and thrive around others. Always get to know more about the people you are surrounded by, and learn their ins and outs. That will be an opportunity to study and learn about them. While dealing with them, they may set some expectations of you, and vice versa. You need to work with them to reach a positive result for both parties and ensure that you are on the same page.

Many people get frustrated because they cannot make things work with others in the way they would like. When things go well for them, then their relationships are good—but otherwise, things don't go well. Having talent and fame don't automatically make people worthy. To become a good, worthy person, be respectful to everyone you meet, regardless of their race, gender, occupation, religion, etc. If you want to be respected, then you must respect others. When you give others everything they want, then you can have everything you want. That is how the equation of happiness and success works.

The activities of your life begin with your desires and thought processes to interact with someone or something. Then you start taking action, which will make you accountable and responsible. You will get results from the actions you perform. You can learn literally anything, using all the latest and greatest techniques and technologies in the world, but if you do not believe in yourself, nothing will happen. It is always possible to achieve more in your life, no matter what you want, when, how, where, or why—you just need the willpower to make your dreams come true. It takes commitment, hard work, dedication, high self-esteem, willpower, and patience to be successful in life. If you have not experienced these things, remember that abundance always comes from a place of willpower, confidence, high self-esteem, happiness, and a can-do attitude. In contrast, scarcity comes from a place of fear of failure, and negative thoughts and attitudes. Hence, a successful life is about how much you are able to make a difference in the lives of others through your own happiness and peaceful mind.

Happiness is a byproduct of good mental and physical health. When you put a massive effort and energy consistently into action for the development of your mental and physical health, you can achieve anything you want in life. This teaches us that you can be bigger than who you are today. In order to have a better future, we need to have a better plan today. No matter what you want to do in your life, you need to have deep study, research, and experience in those areas. Then you can master the needed skills in those areas, as long as you apply your willpower.

Observe yourself, and realize that even if you don't allow other people to give you bad advice, you may still hesitate to learn something that will contribute to your personal growth. You tend to be lazy and say you will do it tomorrow—but tomorrow never comes. If you need to take action, do it now. When you plan to go for a drink at a bar, you do it without the owner of the bar inviting you. When you go to the movies, the theater doesn't invite you—you make that plan yourself. You are capable of making recreational plans, so why don't you plan to develop your personal and professional growth? From my own experience, I learned about a man who was a workaholic but was careless about his health and his family. One day, his wife called him at work and said she needed to rush their daughter to the emergency room. He just yelled at his wife over the phone and said he was busy at work and would not be able to help her. He added that his wife should be able to manage everything herself, although he knew that his wife could not drive. There are many people like him in the world, who do not want to take care of their family. In some cases, people do not want to be responsible for any action they take. You ask someone to do something, but they do not put their heart and soul into it. Sometimes, they fail to keep their promises and commitments and are unable to accept the consequences of their actions. But they suffer the consequences anyway.

You must always make your mental and physical health your first priority. When you are mentally and physically healthy, you can better perform the jobs of being responsible for family, work, and community. The idea is that when you change yourself through your actions, you will influence others to change.

We work every day, as we all are service providers. We get paid for what we sell. All the learning we have in life has earnings with interest. In real life, the future does not get better by hoping, thinking, praying, and dreaming. If we think it will, we will remain in a dream for the rest of our lives. The future gets better only by planning and taking action to enact that plan, today. If we want to be successful in any area of life, we must learn and study in those areas. Doing so will help us to grow socially, economically, personally, and spiritually. Sometimes we do not like what we see around us, and we must learn to change. Anything that we do not want or like in our lives can be changed. In order to be successful, we must always be around successful people, and we can listen to and learn from them.

No successful people come to your door, knocking and offering to help. You need to find them. There are many ways to find good people in your life. You just need to keep exploring through reliable sources, network, and community until you find them. Always stay away from narrow-minded, negative, and cynical people who tend to deceive you, put you down, or humiliate you. Have a great vision, and remain focused on your goals, no matter what the obstacles are. You will succeed, even though you might need to change the plan—but don't change your goals. Successful people are those who are not afraid of a challenge. They face challenges as opportunities and go up from there. They leave their comfort zone, because they know there is no growth in staying where they are. We occasionally need to set aside old habits, no matter how difficult that may be. We let those things go for a good reason—to rise.

We have many inward qualities that we can't see until we use them. If someone says they have never failed, either that's a lie, or they have never tried anything new. There is always room within to become the best version of yourself. Only humans have unlimited opportunities to become what they really want to become. Other things in the world have limitations, but humans don't. Trees are trees, but trees cannot grow past their limitations. The human potential for growth is unlimited. Hence, you must change yourself, in order to be a decent human. Remember, always get inspired to make a difference in the world—don't just be inspired to make a good living. Never, ever let life control you due to pain and frustration. You are capable of controlling your own life and moving forward to the next destination. I always tell people that I don't know if I will live for a few seconds more—or a few minutes, hours, days, months, or years. You must change your reality by changing your mindset, every moment of your life.

Create Your Own Success Story

WE HAVE SEEN and heard a lot of successful people on this planet. By this time, we have learned and understood the secrets behind their success stories. The reality is that they have put considerable time and effort into the vision, mission, passion, and willpower that they translated into action. There are many examples of successful people on earth who started with nothing and have ended up being well-known and rich.

Different people define success in different ways. Some people may define success as being all about expression—having the choice to do what you want to do, go where you want to go, be who you want to become. Others define success as having everything you need in life. Personally, I define it as a process of achieving results from hard work and dedication toward your desired short- and long-term goals, without negatively affecting your mental and physical health, and/or your family and social life.

Although being successful is a process of going through all sorts of obstacles, external distractions, internal pressure, and other problems, you won't get there if you do not have willpower, as well as all the skills you need. This allows you to know and understand what, where, when, how, and why to do things.

Imagine that you wake up full of energy some days, which makes you feel like doing something more meaningful than what you have done in the past. Some days, you wake up and feel you have no energy at all to do anything. Those days are the days when you must take action to make changes in your life. I see many people who simply don't do anything on days when they don't feel like it. In my opinion, that's a roadblock to success.

No one in the world was born destined for success. Everyone was born as a normal human. Those who succeeded knew and learned about successful people around the world. They studied, read books, and researched. They started attending conferences organized by those successful people. Eventually, they also decided to become successful. They developed habits to encourage success. They also had days when they weren't in the mood—when they were frustrated, distracted, doubtful, negative, and suffering from low self-esteem. They had the same pain and fear of scarcity as normal people have. These things are a part of human life. I am sure we all have such moments. What is important is to stay focused, on those days when we have to go through painful moments, feel overwhelmed by financial problems, are insulted and humiliated by people, and face other difficult situations. Those are powerful defining moments toward achieving success. That is because when you're at your lowest and most frustrated point, that is when you have to stand up for yourself and move forward.

Ever since childhood, we have heard the expression "no pain, no gain." There is pain in every aspect of life, but we gain in the future. We need to emerge from our comfort zone, which pulls us toward the path of success. The huge difference between you and someone successful is hard work and dedication. You cannot expect earning without learning and experience. This is another component of the path to success.

Anything you want in life requires giving something in exchange. You always sacrifice something to become better.

Success follows. Each of these actions asks you to break yourself into pieces so that you can reshape your mindset in a better form.

When you really want to succeed, you must set up the self-discipline of being willing to do whatever it takes to get there. You must completely dedicate yourself and work for hours every day, just to get closer to your destination. You must stay focused on your goal, without being distracted by your internal or external environment. Make sure that nothing can change your mind and you are 100% committed to spending time, effort, and energy on achieving your goals. At the end, getting up early in the morning and staying up late will pay off. You will become successful in your chosen field, and that will be the greatest reward of reading this book. May God bless you with a long, peaceful, happy, healthy, and prosperous life.

----------------------------The End----------------------------

CPSIA information can be obtained
at www.ICGtesting.com
Printed in the USA
LVHW031532230121
677292LV00002B/3